IN-HOUSE TEAM

Editor: Mike Toller

Features editor: Alexi Duggins

Senior editorial assistant: Joly Braime

Editorial and production assistant: Alix Fox

Editorial assistance: Anton Tweedale, Claire Gardiner, Kelsey Strand-Polyak, Katy Georgiou

Designer: Sarah Winter

Design assistance: Caitlin Kenney, Sara Gramner

Picture research: Alex Amend

Production consultant: Iain Leslie

Web editor: Cameron J Macphail

National ad sales: Sue Ostler, Zee Ahmad

Local ad sales: Catherine Burke

Distribution: Nativeps

Financial controller: Sharon Evans

Managing director: Ian Merricks

Publisher: Itchy Group

© 2007 Itchy Group

ISBN: 978-1-905705-15-3

Photography: Ross Williams, Bas Driessen, Chris Grossmeier, Mario Alberto, David Tett, Dorrottya Verses, Selma Yalazi Dawani, Tim Ireland, Destination Bristol

Illustrations: Tom Denbigh, Si Clark, Joly Braime

Cover illustration: Si Clark (www.si-clark.co.uk)

Itchy Group
White Horse Yard
78 Liverpool Road
London, N1 0QD
Tel: 020 7288 9810
Fax: 020 7288 9815
E-mail: editor@itchymedia.co.uk
Web: www.itchycity.co.uk

☐☐☐☐☐☐☐☐☐☐☐

Welcome to Itchy 2007

You lucky thing, you. Whether you've bought, borrowed, begged or pinched it off your best mate's bookshelf, you've managed to get your mucky paddles on an Itchy guide. And what a guide it is. If you're a regular reader, you're probably already impressing your friends with your dazzling knowledge of where to head for a rip-roaring time. If, on the other hand, you're a trembling Itchy virgin, then get ready to live life as you've never lived it before. We've spent the last year scouring Bristol for the very best places to booze, cruise, schmooze, snooze and lose ourselves to the forces of pleasure. As ever, we've made the necessary, erm, sacrifices in the name of our research – dancing nights away, shopping 'til we flop and of course, eating and drinking more than we ever thought possible. But we're still alive, and now we're ready to do the whole lot again. Come with us if you're up for it – the first round's on us...

KEY TO SYMBOLS

🕐 Opening times

🍴 Itchy's favourite dish

🍷 Cost of a bottle of house wine

💷 Admission price

Welcome to Bristol

Itchy Bristol would like to warmly offer you our congratulations. If you're reading this, not only are you almost certainly either in or planning to visit the greatest city in the West Country, you've also got your mitts on its greatest guidebook.

Allow this pocket-sized piece of perfection to be your guide to Bristol (or Brizzle as locals call it – or at least that's how the charming local dialect often forces you to say it) and we guarantee you'll trip over all the city's little gems without treading in any of its, er, less savoury venues. Flip to any page and you'll find a unique, painfully honest, appraisal of all that this incredible city has to offer the Bristolian adventurer.

And what a city it is. You name it, we've got it. Well, ok, strictly speaking that's not true. There probably aren't a huge amount of dayglo orange spacecraft around good ol' Brizzle, say, but when there are so many great places to go out, who needs 'em, eh?

What with the city's thoroughly questionable history of slave-trading, you mightn't think that it has too much to offer in the way of heritage. However, don't forget Brunel's awe-inspiring suspension bridge, plus in terms of the contemporary, Banksy's subversive graffiti's doing its bit to help make our walls utterly unique. Home to the Bristol Old Vic, it's about the best place outside London for theatre, and the newly-redeveloped Arnolfini arts centre and Watershed complex ensure that we're at the forefront of modern art as well as a hub for the finest in independent theatre and performance.

The city's pretty nifty for shopping too – as well as all the typical outlets at Cribbs Causeway, there's a breathtaking selection of boutiques, vintage vendors and craft shops. There's also a veritable feast of restaurants for you to choose from, ranging from the critically-acclaimed Glassboat to the fantastically quirky Thali Café. For drinks, try Browns for cocktails overlooking the almighty Wills Building, and, of course, no visit to the city is complete without sampling some hardcore West Country cider at the infamous Coronation Tap.

But that's enough from us about the wonders of Bristol, don't take our word for it: go on, get out there and discover it for yourself. Just make sure that you take us along for the ride too…

Introduction

One day in Bristol

Ah, the eternal quandary of so much to do, so little time. Given just one day in Bristol, how do you get the best out of what the West Country's most versatile and diverse city (yes, that's us) has to offer? Well, for a start you're going to have to be pretty goddamned good at multi-tasking, because there's a hell of a lot to do. Anyway, enough of the religious talk, let's check out what to do in Brizzle in just 24 hours.

First off – hit the shops (not literally, lest ye fancy a set of broken knuckles and some serious enmity from shop owners). A far cry from the soulless grey chain stores of Broadmead, St Nicholas Market makes a good starting point. The market on Corn Street adopts Dolly Parton's working practices by opening Mon–Sat, 9am–5pm, and has four separate areas, each a treasure trove of fun and unique goodies. What a way to make a living. We particularly like the Glass Arcade's mouth-watering food market, with a tantalising selection of snacks and other nibbles.

Having sated your appetite and your inner magpie, head along the waterfront to check out the unmissable attraction that is the Arnolfini. This boutique/arts centre/gallery offers a quick and refreshing shot of culture in the middle of the city, and with its regularly rotating cycle of visiting exhibitions it always makes for an intriguing afternoon. And despite it having a name that makes it sound like it's owned by a mafia don, there's nothing even remotely shady about it. The lovely people that run it are a real bunch of goodfellas, you see.

Next on the agenda is taking a leisurely stroll to @Bristol for some interactive exhibition fun, which is especially good for big kids. Never feel ashamed to connect with the child within, says Itchy. Press all the right buttons, then take a quick trek up Park Street to Brandon Park and its chief attraction, Cabot Tower, commemorating John Cabot's 1497 voyage to America. The tower, erected in 1897, offers a unique perspective on the city as well as a welcome rest for the weary. This interesting local monument was primarily used for flag signalling back in the day. Just something we thought we'd (ahem) flag up to you. Don't worry, there's plenty more-se gems left to come inside too...

Finally, having worked up a nice afternoon thirst, settle yourself down on the steps of Browns for early evening drinks (assuming it's summer – Bristol's climate isn't the mildest in the depths of December). It's a joy for cocktail watchers and people lovers alike. Or maybe that should be the other way round.

Two days in Bristol

For starters, you'll need somewhere to stay. Try the Berkeley Square Hotel off the Clifton Triangle, for easy access to the many delights of Clifton Village. If you're looking for somewhere a bit more cheap and cheerful, look no further than the YHA Youth Hostel, right in the middle of the bustling Waterfront area.

If you're out in Bristol, you've got to look the part. Shop in the eclectic (but pricey) range of outfitters along Park Street, or try the vintage shops on the Gloucester Road. Don't miss BS8's fashion with a twist, and Repsycho's Retro Superstore is a must.

If it's sunny, head to the Clifton Suspension Bridge to enjoy the fabulous view over the city. Just don't look down; it's over a gorge. Recover afterwards with a drink on the terrace at the Avon Gorge Hotel, or in the (fairly likely) event of rain, try the Architecture Centre for a bit of modern design – some might find it a little far-out, but the shop's very cool.

If all that exertion's made you hungry, eat at Fishers for fresh, reasonably-priced seafood. Then, round off the perfect two days at the legendary Coronation Tap, experiencing the evils of Exhibition cider. It's only served in half pints – one sip and you won't be asking why.

Eat

Eat

CAFÉS

All the Tea in China

115 Coldharbour Road

(0117) 909 0357

If you sympathise with Arthur Dent in *The Hitchhiker's Guide to the Galaxy*, travelling across the universe in desperate search of a decent brew, then this might just be your idea of heaven. You get to choose from a huge range of exotic teas, and once you've made your selection, your cuppa is served in a very nifty 'magic filter'. As if that's not enough, you're also issued with your very own tea timer to make sure it doesn't get stewed. Perfect if a good brew is your answer to life, the universe, and everything.

🕐 *Mon–Sat, 9am–5.30pm*

Blue Juice

39 Cotham Hill

(0117) 973 4800

This outstanding coffee and sandwich shop specializes in yummy quesadillas and also does an excellent organic bacon sarnie. The sort of place that makes you feel happier and healthier just by stepping inside. There's a wide choice for vegetarians and enough freshly-made smoothies and juices to keep you on a vitamin high for weeks. If all that fruit sounds a bit too healthy the chocolate brownies are the best Itchy's had. We also love the hyper-friendly (and in fact just plain hyper) staff working here, who are a great advert for the benefits of those blended beauties.

🕐 *Mon–Fri, 8am–4pm; Sat, 9am–4pm*

🍴 *Black bean and cheese burrito, £3*

Bar Chocolat

19 The Mall, Clifton

(0117) 974 7000

Aaaah. Itchy often finds itself caught in a little daydream about the chocolatey wonder that is Bar Chocolat. It's like someone put Willy Wonka's chocolate factory right in the middle of Clifton and then added a load more cocoa-rich sprinkles and marshmallows on top for good measure. Three flavours of hot chocolate, cakes the size of doorstops, enough calories in one visit to keep you going through a seven-month famine; the only thing missing is Johnny Depp with a creepy voice and top hat.

🕐 *Mon–Sat, 9am–6pm; Sun, 11am–5pm*

🍴 *Hot chocolate, small, £1.90; large, £2.80*

Boston Tea Party

75 Park Street

(0117) 929 8601

The year is 1773. Angered by increased taxation, Bostonian colonists destroy £10,000 worth of tea by throwing it into Boston Harbour rather than allowing the ships to unload their cargo. What a waste. But it is important to remember we can learn from history. And in Bristol we find proof that we have. The year is 2007 and Bristol's Boston Tea Party is the finest way to put all that tea-wasting nastiness behind us. A cosy haven for char-drinkers, snuggle into the sofa with a huge wedge of cake and you'll struggle to believe a brew could ever have been the cause of any strife.

🕐 *Mon–Wed, 7am–7.30pm; Thu–Sat, 7am–10pm; Sun, 9am–7.30pm*

Café Delight

189 Gloucester Road

(0117) 944 1133

It may sound like the sort of generic, Lidl-brand instant coffee your mum keeps in the back of the cupboard to give to workmen, but no matter how miserable you are or how rainy it is outside, the bright décor makes it hard not to smile immediately upon entering Café Delight. Furthermore, the array of usual café fare on offer is wide, with many different breakfast options, including more than one vegetarian choice and healthy alternatives such as muesli. Also, their homemade fruit juices and smoothies are a hangover life saver. A delight it certainly is.

☻ *Mon, 9am–5pm; Tue–Sat, 9am–9pm; Sun, 9.30am–3.30pm*

☺ *The fat breakfast, £4.80*

Cake

1b Pitville Place,

Cotham Hill

(0117) 973 2007

The large pink letters on the shop front say it all really: Cake is as Cake does, and in this case, it does rather well. There's coffee, sandwiches and everything else you'd expect from a regular café, but few can resist the 'delicious, massive cup of frothy hot chocolate and freshly-baked cupcake' option. The baked morsels come in a variety of mouth-watering flavours and look as good as they taste, though chances are you'll walk out with more than you bargained for since they do a takeaway service as well.

☻ *Mon–Sat, 8am–6pm*

☺ *Cake, £1.50*

Fried and tested

Breakfast is the most important meal of the day and in Bristol you're spoilt for choice; for the authentic greasy spoon experience and proper cheap prices, try **The Friary** (9 Cotham Hill) for atmosphere. Meateaters fare particularly well here, and though the walls downstairs may be as greasy as the breakfasts, the casual and friendly vibes disguise a little of the oiliness. **Café Delight** (189 Gloucester Road) offers everything from fry ups to nurse you after a rough night to smoked salmon and poached eggs with pesto dressing for those looking to keep their arteries a bit clearer. If the latter approach appeals, you'll like **Oppo** (72 Park Street). It's a healthy alternative and a grand way to pretend you're fit in the morning before the rest of the day catches up with you.

Eat

The Friary Café

9 Cotham Hill

(0117) 973 3664

There is something undeniably homey and warming about the hardwood tables, nice white tea mugs and endearingly pissed off staff at The Friary Café. Boasting the runniest scrambled egg Itchy's had in a long while and fairly tasty fry-ups, it's certainly a passable breakfast stop-off and we've spent many a happy hour sitting in here poring over the sports pages at the weekend. It has particularly good chip butties, which will put a nice solid grounding in your stomach and hopefully bury the torment of last night's heavy one.

☻ Mon, 9am–4.30pm; Tue–Fri, 9am–7pm; Sun, 10am–3pm

❶ Breakfast, £3.65

La Ruca Café

89 Gloucester Road

(0117) 944 6810

This cosy little establishment offers a selection of hearty fair-trade nosh with a Mexican twist, most of which is made using the same stuff as is sold in the wicked little shop downstairs. We reckon the staff are the loveliest in the whole of the South West and are always willing to accommodate even the pickiest vegan. There's still the option of a good full English brekkie if the thought of chowing down on spicy veg first thing in the morning makes you go green around the gills. A friendly home from home for the hip and hippies alike, plus you can eat safe in the knowledge that you're doing your bit for world justice.

☻ Mon, 9am–8pm; Tue–Sat, 9am–5.30pm

Havana Coffee

37a Cotham Hill

(0117) 973 3020

It's not that Havana does anything remarkably different to any other café in Brizzle, it's just that it does everything properly. Good, strong coffee? Tick. Nice, fresh sarnies? Tick. Tasty, filling breakfasts? Tick. Great location bang in the middle of Cotham Hill ideal for people watching? Yes, yes, you get the picture. No complaints with this one at all. Havana might lack some of the kooky individuality of other coffee places lining Cotham Hill but in our opnion it's an upstanding member of Bristol café society, and we'd be at a loss without it. We're Havana other, please.

☻ Mon–Fri, 8am–5pm; Sat, 9am–5pm; Sun, 10am–5pm

Magic Roll

3 Queens Row, Triangle South, Clifton

(0117) 922 1435

Itchy loves Magic Roll. Real, genuine, head-over-heels love. The idea of made-to-order sandwiches isn't new, but then again, these aren't sandwiches – they're Magic Rolls. Just ask for the works and you'll get a Turkish flatbread stuffed with everything under the sun, plus your choice of sauce – you'll never buy lunch anywhere else again. They also do breakfast, including tasty porridge. It's a teeny-tiny place so takeaway is the name of the game – you leave with a little paper bag full of magic and a big, big smile.

☻ Mon–Wed, 8.30am–6pm; Thu–Sat, 8.30am–4pm & 5pm–3am

❶ Magic roll, £3.50

Oppo

72 Park Street (entrance via Park Street Avenue)
(0117) 929 1166

Oppo's a fairly recent addition to the Bristol café scene, and is fitting in a treat. A nice breakfast/lunch stop, the place has the ability to utterly confuse you – no flights of stairs when you enter but you end up on the first floor overlooking Park Street. The mind boggles, and Itchy suspects some sort of jiggery-pokery. Less mysteriously, Oppo also has live music most Saturday lunch times and, best of all, a built-in record shop. A more imaginative combination than sticking a Coffee Republic in the basement of an HMV.

🕐 *Mon–Wed, 8am–6pm; Thu, 8am–10pm; Fri–Sat, 8am–6pm; Sun, 9am–5pm*
🍴 *French toast and roasted vegetables, £3.50*

The Prom

26 The Promenade, Gloucester Road
(0117) 942 7319

A Gloucester Road staple, with outside tables a definite draw in summer. The menu is wide-ranging and you'll be thoroughly chick-peeved if you miss the outstanding homemade hummus. By night there's a wide array of musical acts, plus the legendarily tricky Tuesday pop quiz and Sunday acoustic session. Itchy suggests a visit simply to catch the excellently titled tribute act, Sgt Pepper's Lonely Dartboard Band. We'd tell you they do Queen covers but you're just not going to fall for it.

🕐 *Food, Mon–Fri, 11am–5.30pm; Sat, 10am–5.30pm; Sun, 10am–4.30pm*
🍴 *Homemade beef burger, £5.95*
💰 *£8.30*

Pieminister

24 Stokes Croft
(0117) 942 9500

They don't serve mushy peas, you know. They're 'minty peas, crushed with white wine'. And the pies have got fancy stuff in them too: goats' cheese, chorizo, Thai green curry. If your knowledge of pies extends little further than a Ginster's bought from a petrol station, then much-needed salvation is at hand in the shape of the pie mecca that is Pieminister. Don't scoff, this is much more than a fancy makeover for a snack classic. The décor is a bit on the utilitarian side but you probably won't be paying attention to anything other than what's on your plate.

🕐 *Mon–Sat, 11am–7pm; Sun, 12pm–4pm*
🍴 *All pies, £2.95*

Eat

Shaken Stephen's

88 Park Street

(0117) 316 9269

We're torn on whether the best way to exterminate a gremlin is by microwaving it or whazzing it up in a blender, but we want Stephen on our cretin-crunching tag team for his skills in the latter. He blitzes pretty much anything with his superspeed glory blades, from healthy fruit to every sugar-based treat in Christendom, to make hot shakes, chilled smoothies, or thickies with 97% fat free ice cream. Choose delivery if you just can't prize your arse from the swivel chair, or release your inner rage by wreaking mass jelly baby blended carnage.

☻ *Mon–Fri, 8am–6.30pm; Sat–Sun,*
10am–6pm (changes with seasons)

☻ *Pint of shake, £3.20*

Tiffins

151 St Michael's Hill

(0117) 973 4834

Tiffins is the sort of local takeaway you normally only dream about. The predominantly vegetarian food is all freshly prepared, authentic and dirt cheap. What's more, you can choose as much and as many of the daily-changing options as you can stuff in one of their Tupperware tiffins. But best of all is the couple who own and run the place. They've happily adopted the role of local gurus, doling out sage-like advice and wisdom along with the chapattis and poppadoms. You could come here every other day of your life and not get bored of it.

☻ *Mon–Sat, 12pm–2.30pm & 4pm–9.30pm*

☻ *Vegetarian curry selection, £5*

Take Five Café

72 Stokes Croft

(0117) 907 7502

A leprechaun walks into Take Five Café in scenic Stokes Croft. He shuts the door gently behind him, walks up to the counter and asks for a large strawberry milkshake. 'Coming right up,' says the man behind the till. He embarks on the painfully slow process of preparing the milky beverage. After a few minutes, he stops, and slowly turns around to face the wee green fella. 'You know, we don't get many leprechauns in here,' the man observes. 'At these prices, I'm not surprised,' replies the leprechaun, noting that the café is emptier than a dodo sanctuary, despite it being an otherwise busy lunchtime.

☻ *Mon–Sun, 11am–4pm*

York Café

1 York Place, Clifton

(0117) 923 9656

After years of investigating the effects of large amounts of alcohol the night before, we at Itchy have come to the conclusion that this is probably the best greasy spoon in Bristol. This Clifton institution is the only place to go on a weekend for hangover relief of the first order. Indulge in their monster breakfast, and you get a bit of everything at a very reasonable price. Spend a Saturday morning in here and you'll feel ready to face the world again. And there's something about drinking your orange juice out of a large coffee mug that makes this a truly special dining experience.

☻ *Mon–Sat, 9am–5pm*

☻ *Monster breakfast, £4.80*

RESTAURANTS

The Albion

Boyces Avenue, Clifton

(0117) 973 3522

A popular Clifton haunt for many years, the Albion has recently been transformed into a gastropub of the highest order. The pub bit has been kept downstairs, but the labyrinthine network of upstairs rooms is where the serious gastronomic action takes place. With its exquisite presentation and use of the finest local ingredients, the Albion should be first port of call for any lover of fine food. Save room for pudding.

Ⓒ Mon, 5pm–12am; Tue–Sat, 12pm–12am; Sun, 12pm–10.30pm

Ⓜ Slow braised pork belly, spiced squid, local black pudding, baby leeks, £17

Bangkok House

70 Whiteladies Road

(0117) 973 0409

Itchy have got into trouble before by sticking our nose where it doesn't belong (nevermind other body parts), but we couldn't resist the insistence of our nasal passages when they detected the scent of Thai tom yum soup floating from here. Forget Chanel No.5 or pheromones – wang a bit of that on and you'll be irresistible. The food's a treat for the eyeballs too, and prices excellent, considering portions are more generous than lending your gloves to a leper. Forget gingerbread cottages – houses from Bangkok are clearly far tastier.

Ⓒ Mon–Sat, 12pm–3pm & 6pm–11pm

Ⓜ Roast duck curry, £7.50

Ⓞ £9.50

Bell's Diner

1 York Road, Montpellier

(0117) 9240357

Despite its out of the way location, Bell's Diner is at the high end of Bristol cuisine. Modern European in style, the choice, presentation and cooking are largely faultless, and include some tasty experimental touches. The wine list is extensive and includes some very nice options, and the setting allows you to sit and watch the world outside. Things can start to get pricey when you venture into multiple courses, but sometimes a credit card's gotta do what a credit card's gotta do.

Ⓒ Tue–Fri, 12pm–3pm; Mon–Sat, 7pm–10pm

Ⓜ Main course, around £20

Ⓞ £12.50

Eat

Bosphorus

45–47 Baldwin Street
(0117) 922 1333

Sounds like something you'd find on the periodic table, but the magical elements of Bosphorus in fact make it ideal for a table for two. Serving modern Turkish and a bigger selection of fish than Seaworld, the relatively small fry prices allow you to pick and share a little bit of all sorts. And talking Allsorts, the aroma from the charcoal grill makes your mouth water more than Starburst did back when they were called Opal Fruits, whilst the lavish murals beat staring at the obligatory broken, ugly gas fireplace in your rented lounge.

◉ *Mon–Sun, 12pm–3.30pm & 5.30pm–late*
⑪ *Lokma kebab, £9.95*
◉ *£9.95*

Café Rouge

85 Park Street
(0117) 929 2571

Manages to achieve a distinctly French ambience, while avoiding the curse of most Gallic hangouts: the black-clad, Camus-reading, 'Life is bleak' crowd. Also incorporates lots of the very best 'rouge' things – wine – while sidestepping the less desirable blushes, bank statements and light districts. Spot on for a sophisticated continental breakfast, or if you're after perfect steak-frites, this is as close to eating in a real French restaurant as you're likely to get without the staff being on strike.

◉ *Mon–Fri, 9am–11pm; Sat, 9am–10pm; Sun, 10am–10.30pm*
⑪ *Mussels and chips, £9.95*
◉ *£10.85*

Casa Mexicana

29–31 Zetland Road
(0117) 924 3901

Itchy quite wanted to move to Mexico after our last visit to Casa Mexicana. In fact, it was only a dodgy internet connection that prevented us from booking flights to Mexico City after drinking too many of Casa Mex's rather excellent cocktails. This place is perfect for enjoying authentic food packed tight with bright, bold and exciting flavours. The atmosphere is warm and welcoming; the staff are muy superbo. Come for a taste of true Latin flair – you'll be hard pushed to find a better value restaurant this side of Acapulco.

◉ *Mon–Sun, 6.30pm–10pm*
⑪ *Puerco carnitas, £10.50*
◉ *£11.50*

Eat

FishWorks

128 Whiteladies Road

(0117) 974 4433

Fish lovers of the world unite. Call off the search, you have found your spiritual home. This restaurant and fishmonger is committed to selling and cooking the highest quality fresh fish to an amazing standard. From the salsa verde and garlic mayo served with the bread, to the red and green Tabasco provided with the fish, it's the attention to the little details that makes it worth splashing out on FishWorks. A meal here rarely falls short of perfection and we defy you to find a better plaice anywhere this side of the deep blue sea. Ahem.

🕙 *Tue–Sat, 12pm–3pm & 6.30pm–10.30pm*

🍴 *Whole sea bream baked in sea salt, £16.90*

💰 *£17*

The Glass Boat

Welsh Back

(0117) 929 0704

God invented overdraft facilities for a reason. That reason was The Glass Boat. We're not going to pretend that this place isn't pricey, but it's worth breaking the piggy bank/pawning jewelry/harvesting your organs for a special occasion, because you're guaranteed a top meal here. As the name suggests, The Glass Boat is, indeed, a boat, and the views over Bristol's waterfront, the quite frankly outstanding food and the fine wines make this a unique dining experience.

🕙 *Mon, 12pm–2.15pm & 6.30pm–late;*
Tue–Fri, 7am–9.30am & 12pm–2pm &
6.30pm–late; Sat, 6.30pm–late

🍴 *Venison with neeps and haggis, £18.95*

Eat

Le Monde

The Pavilion,
30 Triangle West, Clifton
(0117) 934 0999

The fun of eating at Le Monde comes in the ordering. Go up to the counter, point out the piece of fish or meat you fancy, choose sauce and side dishes and you're away. You can count on a buzzing atmosphere at this busy spot on the Triangle, and the cooking is certainly up to scratch as well. There are plenty of prix fixe deals available, but nothing beats feasting on the freshly cooked, self-selected goods.

☻ *Mon–Sat, 12pm–10.30pm;*
Sun, 12pm–4pm
🍴 *Dourade baked in coconut, red chilli and coriander, £13.95*
💰 *£12.95*

Lockside

Brunel Lock Road, Cumberland Basin
(0117) 925 5800

Lockside has come a long way since its former incarnation as Sid's Café in *Only Fools and Horses*. Del Boy wouldn't come near this classy joint, owned by siblings Gary and Coral. The food is a nice blend of traditional and contemporary, and locally sourced produce is used where possible. Lockside is a bit out of the way and the advertised views of the Suspension Bridge require a bit of neck craning, but all in all this place is lovely jubbly.

☻ *Mon–Fri, 7am–5pm; Sat, 9am–4pm;*
Thu–Sat, 5pm–11pm
🍴 *Lamb chops with roasted Mediterranean vegetables and sauté potatoes, £9.50*
💰 *£10.75*

Moreish

6 Chandos Road
(0117) 970 6078

The menu might not be a particularly weighty tome but when the food's as good as this, who cares? The waiting staff are friendly without being annoying and the food is served piping hot and delicious. The restaurant is quite tucked away, but worth seeking out if you're going on a date with someone you want to impress. Just don't mention that you had to look it up on MultiMap five times the night before to make sure you didn't get lost.

☻ *Mon–Sat, 10am–10.30pm;*
Sun, 10.30am–9.30pm
🍴 *Salmon steak with olive mash, pak choi, and chilli, ginger and lime dressing, £13.50*
💰 *£11.95*

Mud Dock Café

40 The Grove

(0117) 934 9734

For those of a nervous disposition Mud Dock may not be ideal; mountain bikes hang precariously from the ceiling, apparently for the sole reason that there's a bike shop below the restaurant. Bike shop below = bikes on ceiling. Obvious really, isn't it? Food is the usual Med/Eastern mix but everything's done well and puddings are juicy/creamy/gooey/sticky/totallybloodyyummy exactly when they should be. Everyone seems like they're having loads of fun which makes for a nice friendly atmosphere.

🕐 *Mon–Sat, 9am–11pm; Sun, 10am–5pm*

🍴 *Roasted duck breast, £14.95*

💷 *£11.95*

The One Stop Thali Café

12 York Road, Montpelier

(0117) 942 6687

Being submissive doesn't always have to involve crotchless catsuits and embarrassing rope burns. Abandon yourself to the mercy of the chef at the Thali Café and be rewarded with a big plate of everything curry-based that's been whipped up that day. Save all the 'I've been a very bad kitty' stuff for when you get home though. Actually, if you're looking for guilty pleasure you probably won't find it here; everything is vegetarian or vegan, the wine is organic, and it's all extremely cheap. Pure pleasure in every sense of those two words.

🕐 *Tue–Sun, 6pm–12am*

🍴 *Thali, £6.95*

💷 *£11*

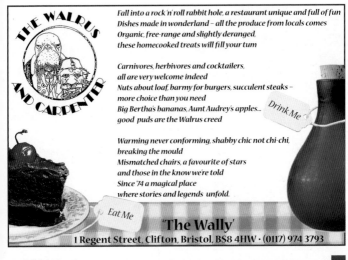

Fall into a rock 'n' roll rabbit hole, a restaurant unique and full of fun
Dishes made in wonderland – all the produce from locals comes
Organic, free-range and slightly deranged,
these homecooked treats will fill your tum

Carnivores, herbivores and cocktailers,
all are very welcome indeed
Nuts about loaf, barmy for burgers, succulent steaks –
more choice than you need
Big Bertha's bananas, Aunt Audrey's apples...
good puds are the Walrus creed

Drink Me

Warming never conforming, shabby chic not chi-chi,
breaking the mould
Mismatched chairs, a favourite of stars
and those in the know we're told
Since '74 a magical place
where stories and legends unfold.

Eat Me

'The Wally'
1 Regent Street, Clifton, Bristol, BS8 4HW · (0117) 974 3793

Eat

Plantation

223 Cheltenham Road

(0117) 907 7932

Plantation has a modern, airy interior and calming music with equally sedate diners. Not really what you'd associate with the tropical, sensuous Caribbean, but hey, we'll let it go. Itchy experimented with the buffet option which, although varied, wasn't really worth the £14.99 price tag. The set menu main courses did, however, look rather good. Go somewhere else if you're in search of a life-changing experience, but for now, we'll stick to downing Malibu with our noses pressed against a fishtank.

☻ Tue–Thu, 6pm–11pm; Fri & Sat, 6pm–11.30pm; Sun, 4pm–9pm

🍴 Jerk chicken, £8.95

🍷 £10.95

Primrose Café

1 Clifton Arcade,

Boyces Avenue, Clifton

(0117) 946 6577

Do you sometimes wish you could spend all day in a restaurant? Well here you can. The Primrose Café starts by serving breakfast, then coffee, including some very fine cakes, then lunch. Come the evening, it turns into a BYOBB* bistro for dinner, which is a rather neat trick, especially as the quality of the food is consistently high throughout. This being Clifton, the bill can turn out a bit high, but the fixed price three course menu is an awesome idea. *The extra 'B' is for 'Brilliance'.

☻ Tue–Sat, 10am–5pm & 7.30pm–9.45pm; Sun, 10am–2.30pm

🍴 Fixed price menu, £17.50

Severnshed

Harbourside, The Grove

(0117) 925 1212

With its extensive bar and dining area, and yummy cuisine that's not too overpriced, Severnshed is a definite highlight of the Bristol waterfront. The outdoor balcony over the river means this is a great place to come spend a summer evening, and the food's not bad either. You can opt for the full à la carte meal or just order a few tapas and nibble away in the bar. Alternatively, skip the food and go straight for the cocktail list, but don't blame us if you suddenly decide to show off your diving skills.

© *Mon–Thu, 11am–12am; Fri–Sat, 11am–2am; Sun, 11am–11pm*

ⓘ *Sirloin steak with fries, £10.50*

❷ *£10.95*

The Walrus & The Carpenter

1 Regent Street, Clifton

(0117) 974 3793

Named after a Lewis Carroll poem, this is pure Wanderland: wander in, and you won't wander out again for several days, finally leaving more stuffed than a taxidermist's and high as a particularly overachieving kite on a Big Bertha's banana cake sugar rush. There's a myriad of miraculous marvels for meaties and veggies, ingredients are organic and locally-sourced, and the rocking family owners come from somewhere magical over the rainbow.

© *Mon–Sat, 12pm–2.30pm & 6pm–11pm; Sun, 12pm–11pm*

ⓘ *Nutloaf with mushroom and watercress sauce, £10.95*

❷ *£14.50*

Zero Degrees

53 Colston Street

(0117) 925 2706

This place is so cool, your tongue would get stuck if you tried licking the walls. It's modern, funky and young, an ideal place to come with your hip mates. Sample the beer from their very own microbrewery including some freaky seasonal mashes e.g. mango beer (interesting indeed), then move on to dinner. Come if you're in the mood for Italian, but like your pizza with a twist. There's a selection of frankly weird but tasty pizza toppings from Peking Duck to Smoky Mexican. So your tongue still gets treated to a novel experience.

© *Mon–Sat, 12pm–12am; Sun, 12pm–11pm*

ⓘ *Thai chicken pizza, £8.25*

❷ *£11.75*

Test of moral fibre

ALRIGHT, SO WE'RE ALL SUPPOSED TO BE EATING ETHICALLY NOWADAYS. BUT WHAT WE WANT TO KNOW IS WHETHER ANY OF THE MONKEYS THAT BANG ON ABOUT THIS STUFF HAVE EVER TRIED IT OUT WHEN PICKING UP SOME POST-PUB STOMACH FILLERS. IT'S A BLOODY NIGHTMARE. OBSERVE:

Illustration by Si Clark, www.si-clark.co.uk

1 Food miles – According to some environmental fascist or other, it's not ecologically friendly to eat stuff that's been flown across the world when you could chomp on courgettes grown much closer to home. Not according to our friendly burger van, however.

Itchy: 'Excuse me, but how many food miles has that quarter pounder done?'

Burger man: 'What?'

Itchy: 'How many miles has it travelled to end up here?'

Burger man: 'Ten miles, mate. Straight from Lidl to this spot.'

Itchy: 'But what about where it came from originally? What about the sourcing?'

Burger man: 'Saucing? I've got ketchup and mustard, you cheeky sod. And it's free, not like him down the road and his "10p-a-sachet" bollocks, now you gonna buy this burger or what?'

'Reckon you could catch enough fish for all the UK's chippies using a fishing rod?'

2 Sustainability – It's not meant to be the done thing to eat fish caught in a way that stops our scaly friends reproducing fast enough to prevent their numbers dropping. Sadly, no-one's told our local chippy.

Itchy: 'Is your cod line-caught?'

Chippy owner: 'Yeah, it's caught mate. How else do you reckon it comes from the sea?'

Itchy: 'No, I'm asking if it was caught using a fishing rod.'

Chippy owner: 'You reckon you could catch enough fish for all the UK's chippies using a fishing rod?'

Itchy: 'Erm, no...'

Chippy owner: 'Right, well there's your answer then.'

Itchy: '…but, you know that you should only really eat fish from sustainable sources don't you?'

Chippy owner: 'Oh yeah? According to who? The media? Reckon all that coke they're on's organic? Produced locally, is it?'

Itchy: 'Well, it's not always possible to consume entirely ethically…'

Chippy owner: 'My point exactly. One cod and chips then is it?'

WHO WHAT WHERE WHEN IS X?

LUXARDO X TEAM COMING TO HOT NIGHTSPOTS NEAR YOU!

GAMES, GIVEAWAYS, COMPETITIONS, PRIZES

WWW.LUXARDOXTEAM.CO.UK FOR MORE ABOUT WHO, WHAT, WHERE & WHEN X IS

LUXARDO
1 8 2 1
SAMBUCA

THE MARK OF SUPERIORITY

Drink

Drink

BARS

All in One
46 Park Street
(0117) 926 5622
Niftily named, this bar, as it provides you with somewhere to eat, drink and dance well into the early hours. Ambient lighting and comfy seats make it ideal to come to with mates for a few bevvies and catch up on the past week's shenanigans. Expect young professionals doing much the same over a vodka lemon and lime or Corona after dinner at the restaurant, because they couldn't be bothered to move on to somewhere else.
◉ *Mon–Sat, 12pm–3.30am; Sun, 12pm–12am; Food, Mon–Sun, 12pm–10pm*
🅢 *£12*

Arnolfini
16 Narrow Quay, Harbourside
(0117) 917 2305
The Arnolfini Bar stands out against its Harbourside neighbours (Yates, Lloyds, et al) as a distinctly sophisticated alternative for the cultured drinker. Artist Bruce McLean's boldly designed interior – complete with funky pop-art light strips and a splendid graphic mural – is worth a look in itself. The drinks here are a bit on the pricey side, but then you get what you pay for. If you want to finish your trip to the gallery in style by sampling their sumptuous cocktail menu, this achingly cool bar is spot on, especially as the art factor seems to act as a shield against chavier types.
◉ *Mon–Sat, 10am–11pm*
🅢 *Cocktails from £4.50*

Amoeba
10 Kings Road, Clifton
(0117) 946 6461
This little gem of a bar, hidden away in Clifton Village, lives a strange double life. By day it's a café where the posh mums and rich students head to sip on their skinny frappu-lattés, but by night it becomes a relaxed bar with a decent range of imported beers on offer. Itchy is also told that you can buy their furniture – a novel but dangerous idea we feel, as it's lovely stuff. We can't help wondering how many 'quick drinks' have ended with people carrying home chairs they never knew they needed.
◉ *Mon–Sat, 9.30am–1am;*
Sun, 10.30am–10.30pm
🅢 *£11*

Bar One 30
130 Cheltenham Road
(0117) 944 2442
'*Sex in the City* has a lot to answer for. These days, it's acceptable for women to sit around, talking openly about sex, but not for a boozer to just offer warm bitter and a packet of stale twiglets. It's all cocktails this and trendy tapas that.' Stop that now grandpa, back to the home for you. Right. Truth is, Bar One 30 offers a massive range of sassy, inventive cocktails and amazing tapas in a trendy setting. Just try and ensure someone else picks up the bill, or you'll have to stay home with gramps next time you want to go out.
◉ *Mon–Thu, 4pm–12am; Fri–Sat, 11am–1am; Sun, 11am–4pm*
🄜 *Mixed tapas plate, £14.50*

Baroque

2 Byron Place, Clifton

(0117) 929 9322

Itchy likes drinking cocktails. Itchy particularly likes drinking lots of cocktails. Consequently, Itchy likes Baroque. The reason for this is extremely simple.There's an extensive menu and accommodating staff who won't call security the second you utter the phrase dreaded by all those who work in the bar industry: 'I know it's not on the board, but I don't suppose you'd mind knocking me up something I first tasted on my travels in the East'. This place has a friendly atmosphere and, best of all, comfy sofas to collapse into when the shaking and stirring gets the better of you.

🕒 *Mon–Thu, 12pm–11pm; Fri-Sat, 12pm–1am*

BsB Waterside

U Shed, Canons Road

(0117) 922 0382

Stylish and in a properly romantic setting, BsB is one of the nicer places on Bristol's Harbourside and is good for lunch in the daytime, drinks in the night-time and most other things in between. The bar is set in the middle of a terribly comfortable seating area from which to watch the wonderful world go by – there's also plenty of amusement to be had watching the steady stream of passing chavs of a Saturday night (those of a nervous disposition, you have been warned).

🕒 *Mon–Thu, 11am–11pm; Fri–Sat, 11am–2am; Sun, 12pm–10.30pm*

🍴 *Chargrilled sirloin steak baguette, £5.50*

💰 *£10*

Drink

Clifton Wine Bar

4 Richmond Terrace, Clifton

(0117) 973 2069

A cosy little nook of a place, with comfy sofas and a laid-back atmosphere, making it perfect for a relaxed glass of red any time of the year. Come summertime, though, the place truly comes into its own with the surprisingly roomy garden and spectacular jugs of iced Pimms. We defy any to suggest a better way of spending an afternoon with a few pals, short of discovering you can turn water into beer just by looking at it. The place attracts a nice mix of locals and students who all get along very nicely, and this is certainly one of the more reasonable places in Clifton.

🕒 *Mon–Sat, 11am–11pm;*
Sun, 11am–10.30pm

The Croft

117–119 Stokes Croft

(0117) 987 4144

One of the best music venues in Bristol, this humdinger is tucked away deep in the bowels of Stoke Croft. It offers live music seven days a week and attracts a colourful mix of locals and the occasional gaggle of intrepid students who've braved the trek out of Clifton to get a flavour of what's going down in the ghetto. They like them guitary and experimental here, so expect boys with funny haircuts jumping around a bit. Don't despair if the tunes aren't quite to your taste, because you can always console yourself with the free pool and retro video games provided for your entertainment.

🕒 *Mon–Sun, 7pm–4am*

Cosies

34 Portland Square

(0117) 942 4110

This place is so cool it's painful, hosting some of the best reggae and d 'n' b nights in the whole of town in its tiny basement setting. It might cost you a pound or so to get in after nine on some nights, but they'll never charge you more than a couple of quid, so you can't really complain. Food here is lush too, with different specials being prepared by the chef each day, plus it's the ideal place to recover from a hangover with a cooked breakfast thanks to its gentle underground lighting and general relaxed feel.

🕒 *Mon–Fri, 10am–2am; Sat–Sun,*
8pm–2am; Food, 10am–2pm
💰 *£9.50*

Ha! Ha! Bar and Canteen

20a Berkeley Square

(0117) 927 7333

Ha! Ha! is solid wood and retro chic. A modern look is matched by its attitude and by its clientele, which ranges from the sharpest suits to scruffy students. Describing itself as a 'Bar & Canteen', it's a place of few pretensions that just happens to serve trendy food and good drinks. Ha! Ha! is roomy and has a nice garden, making it a perfect place to chat and chill, but wind up anything deep and meaniful by evening time, when the pace steps up and the bar can get a bit rammed.

🕒 *Mon–Thu, 11am–11pm; Fri, 11am–12am;*
Sat, 10am–12am; Sun, 10am–10.30pm
🍴 *Posh fish finger sandwich, £5.95*
💰 *£10.95*

Hush Bar

233 Cheltenham Road

(0117) 942 2700

Look past the slightly tacky sign outside, take a leap of faith, and head inside. We think you'll be pleased you did. Once you've reached the bar, you've got a choice of a fairly decent wine and beer or some classic cocktails to sip while you kick back. It's one of those places that's all dark and atmospheric with trendy types having a boogie to some funky music. For a bit of a change from the many, ghastly chain bars of Brizzle, bring a close group of friends, grab yourself a comfy sofas and a drink or three, and wonder whatever happened to Kula Shaker.

© *Wed–Mon, 6pm–12am; Tue, 7pm–12am*

❷ *£12*

Mackies Bar

84 Stokes Croft, Stokes Croft

(0117) 924 9995

Mackie's promote themselves as somewhere to 'chillax', but don't worry, the place lacks next to nothing, least of all warm atmosphere and evening energy that just won't quit, and has no loosening effect on the bowels. You can keep your purse strings tight too. The already-cheap food and drinks have further 15% discounts for students. At night there's a bigger buzz than at a bar mitzvah in a beehive, and the beer garden is jumping in summertime, but Itchy is saving the biggest potion of our love pie for the retro arcade games. The term 'joystick' has never been so apt.

© *Mon–Wed, 12pm–12am; Thu, 12pm–3am; Fri–Sun, 12pm–5am*

Las Iguanas

113 Whiteladies Road

(0117) 973 0730

Ok, so Itchy has four words for you: 'raspberry', 'Martini', 'happy' and 'hour'. Another four words are 'two for one cocktails'. This is pretty much all you need to know about Las Iguanas, other than that this fantabulous offer runs until 7.30pm every night (bar Sundays and Mondays, when happy hour lasts all evening). The next words to spring to mind are 'utterly' and 'trolleyed'. Handily, they also do pretty good Latin-themed grub to line the old stomach before indulging.

© *Mon–Thu, 12pm–3pm & 5pm–11pm; Fri–Sat, 12pm–11.30pm; Sun, 12pm–10.30pm*

⑪ *Xinxim (Brazilian lime chicken), £9.80*

❷ *£12.50*

Drink

MBargo

38–40 Triangle West
(0117) 925 3256

Ideally situated for early drinking before a night at Po Na Na or, erm, the Lizard Lounge (no comment, next question please...) this trendy bar is popular with students and taxpaying types alike. MBargo does share the same style of commercial cool with big hitters like Pitcher & Piano or All Bar One, but the giant leather sofas and moody lighting provide a nicely intimate atmosphere that prevents it from becoming completely soulless. Legendary club nights such as Thank Funk It's Friday also ensure that this bar stands out a little from the crowd.

◉ *Mon–Sat, 12pm–4am; Sun, 12pm–2am*
◔ *£6*

The Park

37 Triangle West
(0117) 940 6101

Trendy bar serving trendy cocktails while trendy DJs spin it up. Get the picture? It's so trendy they even try to serve the most en-vogue food around: Thai. But at the end of the day, trendy is all it really is, and nothing more. It's devoid of character, and on a busy evening you'd be forgiven for forgetting where you were, even before you'd gotten truly stuck into the well-stocked bar. Still, you're swanking it up with the best of them, which can be fun at times, though it hardly makes for the kind of evening you're truly entitled not to remember.

◉ *Mon–Thu, 11am–11pm;*
Fri–Sat, 11am–1am

Mr Wolf's

33 St Stephens Street
(0117) 927 3221

'Noodles, live music, late bar.' Mr Wolf's slogan is informative but doesn't tell you the following: if you leave the venue drunk looking for a cashpoint in the centre of town, you might never find your way back again (all the streets look the damn same around here). The noodles are a little overpriced, but very tasty, and when drunk they'll be all you'll want in the world. The live music ranges from supremely fun and funky to truly dire. Gets packed at night, so arrive early and lounge around gloatingly on your valuable seat.

◉ *Mon–Tue, 6pm–2am; Wed–Sat,*
6pm–4am; Sun, 6pm–12.30am
◔ *£9.95*

Picture House Bar

44 Whiteladies Road
(0117) 973 9302

Next to the old Picture House on Whiteladies Road, this place oozes silver screen sophistication and class. Come and enjoy the sumptuous surroundings and feel like a movie star as you enjoy a drink from their wide selection of exotic but classy cocktails, fine spirits and new world wines. Come for a bit of modern style and glamour in the kind of place where Scarlett Johansson and Jude Law would feel at home. Who knows, you might look so cool that someone will ask you to star in a blockbuster of your own.

◉ *Mon–Sun, 12pm–12am; Food, Mon–Sun,*
12pm–11pm
◔ *£13.50*

Quadrant

2 Princess Victoria Street
(0117) 974 1025

Less 'a glass of the usual' and more 'the finest wines available to humanity', the Quadrant prides itself on its selection of wine and beer. By no means the biggest place in the world (or indeed Clifton), there is an intimate bar and an underground wine cellar catering for the casual drinker and the connoisseur alike. Twinned with the Clifton Sausage down the road, brunch and lunch are also on offer, though the booze rules here, making it a must for those who know their vintages.

🕒 *Mon-Wed, 11am-11pm; Thu-Sat, 11am-12am; Food, Mon-Sat, 11am-4pm*

🍴 *Homemade sausage rolls, £3.50*

🍷 *£13.50*

The Roo Bar

Clifton Down Station, off Whiteladies Road
(0117) 923 7204

Battered chesterfields and distressed–looking wood was clearly the brief when designing the Roo Bar. That's not necessarily a bad thing though, as the overall effect is one of faded comfort, making it a perfect place for a quiet drink and a good gossip. That doesn't apply at all when there's a rugby match on, as this is a great hangout for watching a game, provided you can fit yourself through the door and find a spare quarter-to-half inch of empty floorspace to squeeze into – the atmosphere's electric and the punters go completely bonkers.

🕒 *Mon-Sat, 11am-11pm; Sun, 12pm-10.30pm*

Drink

Stark Bar

168 Whiteladies Road
(0117) 973 9522

When a mummy and a daddy have a special hug, the Stark brings them a multi-floor bundle of joy. Inside, it sparkles with gilt mirrors, chandeliers, and sumptuously terrific tack you'll get utterly stuck on. It has a kitsch-en that prepares delicious foodstuffs, curry and movie nights (with free popcorn), a roof terrace for BBQs in the summer, and more delightful little touches than mummy says daddy ever achieved, even during their very best embraces.

☻ *Mon–Sat, 12pm–11pm; Sun, 12pm–10.30pm; Food, Mon–Sat, 12pm–3pm & 6pm–10pm (Sat, 8pm); Sun, 12pm–8pm*

🍴 *Shredded duck tartine, £6.50*

❷ *£12.25*

Tantric Jazz Café Bar

39–41 St Nicholas Street
(0117) 940 2304

This isn't some sort of kinky sex joint we're afraid, but it's still worth popping along in our opinion. If anyone's still reading after that initial letdown, get yourself over to Tantric Jazz safe in the knowledge that the Sting-alikes will have thrown this book at the wall in a fit of yogic pique and are now trying to control their rage by chanting 'mung... mung... mung...' For those who've made it, there's live jazz music seven nights a week, tasty, cheap tapas and plenty of alcohol to keep your inner finger-snapper well hydrated. Tantric Jazz hits all the high notes for a good night out, especially if you're into staying out late on a Sunday.

☻ *Mon–Sun, 5pm–3am*

Tobacco Factory Café Bar

Raleigh Road, Southville
(0117) 902 0060

This chilled, hip place was founded on surprisingly fervent principles. Don't panic though, no one will be hassling you to sign petitions. The main aim of the complex inside this one-time factory is to support local businesses. And that means tasty beer made just down the road at the small, award-winning Bristol Beer Factory, plus fabulous, freshly cooked Mediterranean-style fodder that hasn't been flown halfway around the world before landing on your plate.

☻ *Sun–Thu, 12pm–11pm; Fri–Sat, 12pm–12am; Food, Mon–Sat, 12pm–3pm & 5.30pm–9pm; Sun, 12pm–4pm & 5.30pm–8.30pm*

❷ *£9.80*

Drink

PUBS

Alma Tavern
18–20 Alma Vale Road, Clifton
(0117) 973 5171

It's a rather fine thing to have a pub with a little theatre in their upstairs room. Now you have the perfect excuse for all the hours you spend in the boozer: 'I'm not getting pissed, I'm enjoying a rich cultural experience' and all that. If you need any more justification, there's an exciting quiz with surreal prizes every Monday. You might even win a toy gun to shut up whoever is still telling you you're spending a bit too much time in this lovely pub.

🕒 Mon–Sat, 12pm–12am; Sun, 12pm–10.30pm; Food, 12pm–9.30pm
🍴 Calves' liver and mash, £12.50

The Bell
21 Alfred Place, Kingsdown
(0117) 922 1006

The Bell has recently fallen victim to the 'refurb = price hike' phenomenon, and the bar list is now both fancy and expensive. That said, the atmosphere remains as friendly as ever, whether you're a local who pops in every night or you've stumbled across the pub for the first time. It's a warm, candlelit haven in the bleak Legoland concretescape of High Kingsdown and for that we are truly thankful. It's also pretty tiny, so be prepared to snuggle up. Cosy, but probably wise to pick your potential drinking buddies carefully.

🕒 Mon–Fri, 12pm–11pm; Sat–Sun, 11am–11pm
🍴 £11

Drink

The Bunch of Grapes

8 Denmark Street
(0117) 987 0500

Tucked away in its own little sidestreet, yet still within spitting distance of the Waterfront, this friendly little boozer is the perfect place for a quiet drink on a weeknight. The walls are covered, and we mean absolutely covered, with posters from every show ever put on in the entire history of the neighbouring Hippodrome. We reckon this is very handy, as it means you shouldn't ever be stuck for a topic of conversation if you decide to bring a particularly boring date here. Just be careful not to take them down to the harbour, in case they, err, trip and fall in.

🄲 *Mon–Fri, 11am–3pm & 5pm–11pm;*
Sat, 11am–11pm; Sun, 12pm–10.30pm

The Cat and Wheel

207 Cheltenham Road
(0117) 942 7862

Ooh, it's a bit of a gem this one. Ropey doesn't even begin to describe the dodgy-looking Cat and Wheel, but nevermind appearances; we think this all adds to the overriding feeling of local charm, and who are we to judge a book by its cover? Once you've made the decision to enter, you'll notice that the pub is split into two separate bars. You can take your pick and either choose to sit on the side with the scary-looking locals or the side with the, err, even more scary-looking locals. Either way, they've got a license and the odd chair. What the hell else are you after?

🄲 *Mon–Sat, 6pm–11pm; Sun, 7pm–10.30pm*

Cadbury House

68 Richmond Road
(0117) 924 7874

The Cadbury has that rare and magical quality that makes it special: a real sense of community that's missing from so many of the bars that people put together out of flatpacks they buy in IKEA these days. Granted, a fair number of this particular community might be dreadlocked crusti-farians, but we won't hold that against them too much. Whether you're sat in the warm cavernous interior or the huge beer garden, you're likely to emerge feeling mellowed out, and that'll just help you to enjoy the weekend DJ sets all the more.

🄲 *Mon–Sat, 12pm–11pm;*
Sun, 12pm–10.30pm
🄰 £7.50

The Clifton

16 Regent Street
(0117) 974 6321

The Clifton used to be endearingly dingy, offering cheap beer to go with the cheap interior. But, in keeping with the standard Clifton treatment of all cosy locals, they've turned all that around, ripping out all the original fittings and sprucing the place up, and yet again jamming up the prices. It's now a thoroughly nice place to go for a chilled out wind-down drink on a weekday evening, although Itchy isn't convinced that it wasn't just as much fun (and a hell of a lot cheaper) before.

🄲 *Mon–Thu, 12pm–12am; Fri–Sat,*
12pm–1am; Sun, 12pm–11pm
🄰 £10

Coronation Tap

8 Sion Place, Clifton

(0117) 973 9617

Known affectionately to its regulars as the 'Corrie Tap', this tucked-away boozer is the perfect starting point for many a bleary-eyed evening adventure. Its landlord is proud owner of the infamous Exhibition Brewery, which makes a cider so strong that it is only sold in half pints and has been known to orchestrate the downfall of many a supper. The Tap is one of Itchy's favourite pubs in Bristol for the playing of rowdy drinking games, not least because it's usually so busy in there that no one will notice when you pass out under the table.

Ⓒ *Mon–Fri, 5.30pm–11.00pm; Sat, 7pm– 11pm; Sun, 12pm–4pm & 7pm–11pm*

Ⓞ *Exhibition cider, £2*

Cotham Porter Stores

15 Cotham Road South

(0117) 903 0689

You'd be forgiven for thinking on first glance that you'd walked into the pub from *American Werewolf in London*; it's the type of place that gives you the feeling the locals will be drawing straws for your shoes while you're in the loo. But get a couple of pints of their vividly orange cider in you and you'll find they're a friendly bunch really. This stuff is knockout. A couple more and you'll be buying the whole pub a round and making wild promises about joining their cricket team. Just steer clear come the full moon.

Ⓒ *Mon–Sat, 12pm–11pm; Sun, 12pm–10.30pm*

Ⓞ *£10.50*

Ye Shakespeare

78 Victoria Street, Bristol, BS1 6DR   (0117) 949 7708

One of Bristol's oldest friends
Since 1636
We've offered pool and darts and warmth
And pints that can't be licked.
The talk you hear of Geri's grub
Ain't Much Ado about Nothing

Homemade favourites, hot and cold, Are the very best of stuffing.
Thurs and Fri there's breakfast too
Each month hosts six guest beers
Are real pubs pure poetry to you?
Then visit Ye Shakespeare

Mon–Wed, 11am–11pm; Thu–Fri, 8am–11pm; Sat, 12pm–11pm; Food, Mon–Sat, 12pm–3pm, breakfast, Thu–Fri, from 8am

Drink

The Elbow Rooms
64 Park Street
(0117) 930 0242

In a prime Park Street location, The Elbow Rooms are the perfect place for a refreshing mid–pub crawl stop-off. We don't recommend going there too early in the evening though, as you'll still be sober enough to think twice about paying the fairly extortionate prices. There is, however, a nice pool area that's popular on weekends, great for both those who enjoy playing the sport, and those who enjoy admiring the arses of fit players as they bend over. Not that we'd ever eye anyone up, of course. You filthy perverts, you.

Mon–Sat, 12pm–2am;
Sun, 12pm–12.30am

The Highbury Vaults
164 St Michael's Hill, Cotham
(0117) 973 3203

Before it was a pub, the Vaults used to be the holding cells where condemned men spent their final days before hanging; if you're a student asking for cashback at the bar you might meet a similar fate. The Vaults is dark and cosy with great food and a sometimes palpable townies vs. students tension. Whichever side of the fence you're on, though, ignore this and enjoy the fantastic heated garden and quality range of ales at the bar. And don't go asking stupid questions without reading the 'Stupid Questions' board first – you have been very warned.

Mon–Sat, 11pm–11pm;
Sun, 12pm–10.30pm

The Hatchet Inn
27 Frogmore Street
(0117) 929 4118

Entering The Hatchet on your average Friday night is perhaps not for the faint of heart. Yet with its strange blend of quaint Elizabethan architecture and pre-ramshackle goth biker bar atmosphere, there is something weirdly, almost perversely, charming about the place. With its very reasonable prices it's also guaranteed to have you headbanging and issuing a victorious war cry of 'Led Zep rules' before the evening is out; even if you go in there a Cliff Richard fan, they'll soon scare you straight.

Sun–Wed, 12pm–11pm;
Thu–Sat, 12pm–2am
Pint of Fosters, £2.10

Hobgoblin
69–71 Gloucester Road, Bishopston
(0117) 940 1611

It's what you'd call an old man's pub. But don't be put off. It does have the dark wood and a few crinkly bidders, but that's what adds to the charm. It's the perfect place to come for a quiet Sunday evening drink, or alternatively, rock up when there's a footie match showing on telly, as The Hobgoblin comes into its own then. Rammed full of people all clambering to see the match and complete with bacon sarnies for sale – it's the next best thing to being there for real. Plus, you can make it to the loo and back at halftime.

Mon–Sat, 12pm–11pm;
Sun, 12pm–10.30pm
£9

The Hope & Anchor

38 Jacobs Wells Road
(0117) 929 2987

After several years in Bristol, it was Itchy's mum (who doesn't even live here) who told us about The Hope & Anchor's amazing beer garden. It was embarrassing for us to have to take her advice. Come summer, the wonderfully shambolic terraced garden is the perfect place to enjoy a drink. Take someone you want to sleep with and, as long as they've never been before, you'll probably get lucky. Provided they didn't hear you getting this tip from your mum.

🕐 Mon–Sat, 12pm–11pm; Sun, 12pm–10.30pm; Food, Mon–Sat, 12pm–10pm; Sun, 12pm–9.30pm
🍴 Sausage and mash, £7
💷 £12.50

Lansdown

8 Clifton Road
(0117) 973 4949

The light and airy Lansdown, with its comfortable chairs and stick-free tables has all the atmosphere of a cosy, traditional pub, but without being dingy. Good quality food and popular open mic poetry nights complete the living room feeling. Of course, it's actually way better than your own living room, which probably doesn't have such a well-stocked bar. The pub pulls a corker in the summer months when it hosts amazing barbecues to be enjoyed outside in the (heated) garden, making the Lansdown a handsdown best bet.

🕐 Mon–Sat, 12pm–11pm; Sun, 12pm–10.30pm
💷 £10.75

Games for a laugh

Fancy playing games while drinking? Add intellectualism to your alcoholism and hit some of Bristol's many pub quizzes. On Monday, the hot quiz ticket is the **Alma Tavern**'s (18–20 Alma Vale Road) student-friendly affair. With prizes ranging from a minute behind the bar to an X-box, you can even win stuff simply for being the noisiest team (Team Itchy still fondly recalls scooping this accolade and winning a rather excellent blow gun). On Sundays, **The Roo Bar** (Clifton Down Railway Station, Whiteladies Road) provides free snacks. As long as you've got a half-decent team you stand a good chance of scooping the £100 prize, making this a bargain night out. Even better, if you can come up with an amusing team name you can bag a free bottle of wine (current

Drink

The Old Duke

45 King Street, City Centre

(0117) 927 7137

The Old Duke, named after legendary musician Duke Ellington, is Bristol's home of live jazz. Jazz is not, however, The Old Duke's only winning attraction. The outdoor seating makes it perfect for the two lazy summer evenings we get every year, and their wide selection of spirits (yes, boys and girls, we've spent a night on the absinthe here, and yes, it is in fact the devil's own piss) goes to further prove why time spent in the Old Duke makes for an excellent night on the tiles (and one hell of a liver-twistingly painful morning after).

🕒 *Sun–Thu, 12pm–11.30pm;*
Fri–Sat, 12pm–12am

The Rising Sun

86–90 Gloucester Road, Bishopston

(0117) 989 2471

Now, this is a typical 'Scream' pub in every sense. If you went in there to spend a sober-ish evening it'd make you scream in horror. If you saw the ugly lack of atmosphere in there during the day when the place isn't crammed to the brim with braying drunken lunatics cheerily humiliating themselves, it'd make you wail with the despair of aesthetic paralysis. Given this basic premise however, there's many a fun and lively night to be had, particularly on Monday night when everything costs £1. Nice mix of people, in that students from both universities attend, as well as local folks, and all get wasted together.

🕒 *Sun–Mon, 12pm–12am*

The Prince of Wales

5 Gloucester Road

(0117) 924 5552

The Prince of Wales welcomes its diverse group of regulars: students, workers and the rest of the Gloucester Road art pack all happily drink shoulder to shoulder here. There's not much seating space, but who cares when it's friendly enough to be able to chat at the bar? A good choice of tunes, heated outside seating and excellent organic food make this an upbeat place for a pint or three. Beware the unisex toilets, though; many a confused person has been left wondering if they've wandered into the wrong cubicles after a few too many.

🕒 *Mon–Sat, 12pm–11pm;*
Sun, 12pm–10.30pm
💰 *£10.95*

Robin Hood

56 St Michael's Hill

(0117) 929 1334

One of Itchy's cohorts fell down some steps here after the dangerous combination of playing drinking games and being stupid had got the better of her. The regulars justifiably laughed. While it's not often that outsiders penetrate this spot (maybe something to do with the very steep hill this pub's on?), when they do they're warmly received and will probably find it near impossible to leave (that pesky hill seems to get steadily steeper the more booze you consume).

🕒 *Mon–Thu, 12pm–3pm & 5pm–11pm;*
Fri–Sat, 12pm–11pm; Sun, 12pm–10.30pm;
🍴 *Roast dinner, £6.50*
💰 *£11.50*

The Three Sugar Loaves
2 Christmas Steps
(0117) 929 2242

A refurb has left this 17th century pub with something of a split personality: downstairs is always warm and cosy and drinking pints of Hoegaarden by the fireside makes for memories to treasure. However, upstairs is home in the evenings to an under-populated semi-dancefloor and a miffed looking DJ. Itchy's advice is to stick to the comfy sofas below and the beaming smiles of the friendly bar staff and you'll feel like you're having a beer served to you in your own living room (or someone else's nicer living room if yours is a shithole that hasn't been cleaned in years).

◉ *Mon–Fri, 12pm–12am; Sat, 4.30pm–1am; Sun, 12pm–6pm*

The White Bear
133 St Michael's Hill
(0117) 929 7265

The guy that owns this pub probably doesn't like authority very much. Luckily, he's decided that the best way of expressing his displeasure over the mechanisms of a modern democratic state is to offer really cheap booze on Mondays and Thursdays. Sell enough doubles and mixers for two quid and surely the government will soon topple. The students who flock here don't give a monkey's about his politics, they just want to drink quadruple vodka and cokes in pint glasses. After a couple of them, it's you, not the state, that is ready to collapse in a ruined heap.

◉ *Mon–Sat, 12pm–12am; Sun, 12pm–10.30pm; Food, 12pm–2.30pm*

Drink

The White Hart

54–58 Park Row

(0117) 945 6060

Cleaner and more nicely decorated than most 'Scream' pubs, this is still somewhere you probably wouldn't bother with unless you were looking for a cheap drink (with the emphasis being on cheap). Hence the clientele being made up entirely of students and fresh-faced skater-types. That said, they do good cheap food as well, and it's an alright place in the daytime when it's not too crowded. Plus the staff are always friendly, and they have MTV and pool tables to keep you amused. Get yourself a yellow card and join the youthful hordes.

☺ Mon–Sat, 11am–11pm; Sun, 12pm–10.30pm; Food, Mon–Sat, 12pm–7pm; Sun, 1pm–7pm

Ye Shakespeare

78 Victoria Street

(0117) 949 7708

Friends, Romans, countrymen, lend us your ears; we need another orifice to pour our pints into. It's been standing for nearly 400 years, which is around 5.25 million hours longer than you'll manage after downing the half-dozen guest ales on offer. There's darts, a pool table, and we love their policy of serving breakfast just on Thursdays and Fridays; that's two mornings tucked into one of the Macbeth-t full Englishes around, and another five tucked up for a lie-in without feeling like we're missing out. Far too good to risk getting Bard.

☺ Mon–Wed, 11am–11pm; Thu–Fri, 8am–11pm; Sat, 12pm–11pm; Food, Mon–Sat, 12pm–3pm (breakfast, Thu–Fri, from 8am)

The Woods

1 Park Street Avenue

(0117) 925 0890

As the *Teddy Bears' Picnic* taught us: 'If you go down to the woods today, you're in for a big surprise'. That's certainly the case in the case of these Woods, resplendently decorated in animal skulls and insects and with a funky-kitsch granny's attic-style upstairs balcony. They also have a very cosy heated outdoor garden, stupidly late opening hours and every type of whisky imaginable, so the surprise is certainly a nice one. Just don't drink so much that you end up leaving barer than when you came in. You won't be able to bear the shame.

☺ Sun–Thu, 4pm–2am; Fri, 4pm–4am; Sat, 4pm–6am

Stay regular

Illustration by Joly Braime

AIN'T NOTHIN' QUITE LIKE STEPPING INTO A BAR AND BEING GREETED AS ONE OF THEIR OWN. HERE'S ITCHY'S GUIDE TO BECOMING AS REGULAR AS CLOCKWORK SOMEWHERE NEW

1 Learn the name of the publican's partner/pet/mum – Take a couple of mates and stand at the bar within earshot of the publican and engage in the 'what would your porn name be?' game (combine your pet's name with your mum's maiden name). After a while, get the publican to join in, and make up some new variants designed to extract info about the names of spouses, dad, etc. Next time you walk in, you'll be able to greet them with a friendly, 'Alright Dave, how's Sandra doing?'

2 Have your own pint mug – Take a vessel and ask them to keep it behind the bar for you. Then whenever you walk in, you can sup your beverage in style. You may want to save this for the second visit.

3 Know the pool rules – If they've already got a set of rules in place, learn what they are, loiter near the table and make sure you pounce upon any infraction to loudly proclaim 'That's not how we do things in here'. If there are no house rules, even better – make some up, don't tell anyone what they are, and then soon everyone'll need to ask you before playing.

4 Start a cribbage team – Unless the pub in question's populated by incontinent octogenarians, there's no chance that they'll have one. Get a 'Captain' T-shirt, and swan round asking randoms if they're ready for the big match. They'll have no idea what you're talking about, allowing you to explain your importance to the pub community.

5 Take a dog – Everyone loves a dog. Well, except asthmatics. But who cares about them? Those guys are already having enough of a wheeze.

SHROOM WITH A VIEW

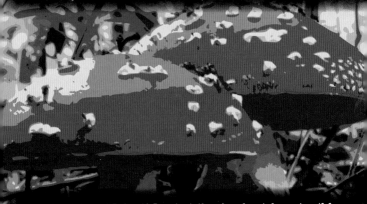

See the sights of Bristol! Psychedelics, fungi, salvia, aphrodisiacs, chillers, thrillers, laughing gas, pills, potions, smoking mixes and hangover fixes – when it comes to legal, herbal and alternative highs, Laughter Promotions have got it covered.

- Constantly sourcing the latest and greatest experiences, from traditionally Shamanic dried Peruvian Torch Cactus, through scores of spores, maxers and relaxers, to pills direct from legit New Zealand labs.
- Complete laughing gas party kits and stalls for hire
- Know what you're getting – and get it fast. Orders placed before 1.30pm will be with you the next day
- Quality products developed to maximise sensation and minimise harm, at great prices. All items available wholesale
- Responsible advice on the mild to the wild
- 100% legal, 100% incredible

Our website has all the info and options you need – plus, type in ITCHY1 at the checkout and receive 10% off your purchases.

Dance

Dance

CLUBS

Baja

Canons Road, The Watershed

(0117) 922 0330

Baja is probably what Dante had in mind when he dreamt up the seventh circle of hell. Wednesdays and Fridays are the nights that really define the place, when it plays host to Wedgies, an almighty student cheese-fest. Leading the way to oblivion is the somewhat odious DJ, Mr Wedge, who delights in organising topless contests among young student ladies. Anyone order a copy of *Girls With Low Self-Esteem, Vol IV*?

☺ *Mon, VodSoc, 10pm–2.30am, £2, NUS only; Wed & Fri, Wedgies, 10pm–2.30am, £3–£3.50; Thu, Ministry of Cheeze, 10pm–late, £2–£4 after; Sat, 10pm–3am, £2–£5*

The Black Swan

438 Stapleton Road, Eastville

(0117) 939 3334

Not for the faint-hearted or even the reasonably brave-hearted; in fact you'll be giving William Wallace a run for his money if you're not quaking on your first trip to the Swan. The supremely dirty drum 'n' bass, mud-carpeted (well, hopefully it's mud) toilets and low ceilings dripping with sweat attract a crowd in dire need of a good talk with Frank. But dancing round the campfire with dreadlocked flame-spinning strangers as the sun comes up is tho kind of experience that you're not likely to have every day of the week. Well, unless you have a fairly serious problem, that is.

☺ *Opening times and days vary*

🎫 *£10 advance booking; £12 on door*

Different strokes

Fancy expanding your horizons? Brizzle's got plenty of different stuff to offer. **Stutter** is one of the youngest faces on the Bristol alternative scene; it's just moved to club-on-a-ship **Thekla** (0117 929 3301) but the main room still spins indie/electro and the emo room is still jammed with walking Myspace profiles and brilliant tracks you won't hear anywhere else. For something a little (alright, a lot) more mainstream try chain indie night **Fat Poppadaddy's at Po Na Na** (0117 925 6225) on Tuesdays. The finest alternative night in the city is the small but mighty **Wonky** (0776 372 3454). The playlist is cool and exciting and catches you off guard in the way only an indie/electro/80s night can. It's sweaty, rammed, and the official description is 'for homos who hate hard house' but if you're bothered by the gay factor then you're losing out, loser.

Blue Mountain

2 Stokes Croft

(0117) 924 6666

They call it the 'world famous' Blue Mountain club. Who exactly 'they' are we don't know, but even calling this place 'Bristol famous' would possibly be overstating things somewhat. Still, if you haven't been to Blue Mountain and are of the d 'n' b/breaks persuasion, make the trip. Venetian Snares, Rennie Pilgrim and Jon Kennedy have all popped up recently and come Christmas, free parties offer lots of exciting music for very few of your English pennies (alright, maybe we mean pounds). In summer, there's an open-air terrace if the dance floor gets a bit too much for you.

Ⓒ *Mon–Sat, 10pm–5am*

Ⓔ *£6 before 11, £8 with flyer, £10 without*

Laughter Promotions

www.laughterpromotions.com

(0117) 941 5836

Searching for pot pourri to add that quaint, traditional shamanic look to your downstairs loo? Try the dried Peruvian torch cactus. After some psychedelic flora to pep up the parched pansy arrangement in your window box? Get your Hawaiian woodrose seeds here. If you need gas, forget Transco and log on to www.laughterpromotions.com, where by tapping in ITCHY1 at the checkout, you can get 10% off. Interested in phonetics? You'll note extensive use of the letter 'E' on this site. Are we sidestepping more than an attempt to break the world line dancing record? Of course not. There's not mushroom here for that kind of behaviour.

Dojo Lounge

12–16 Park Row

(0117) 925 1177

Dojo is the kind of underground club where the words 'dark' and 'dingy' generally tend to be used in a complimentary way. The DJs play an inspiring mix of d 'n' b, r 'n' b and hip-hop tastier than raw cookie dough, and Dojo's intimate (read packed and sweaty) dancefloor and cosy seating areas give way to a smoky heated outdoor section with heaps of comfy sofas to collapse in. Head into the open air for the perfect way to unwind after a long night of getting down to some top choons leaves you more tired than Itchy's collection of puns circa 1999.

Ⓒ *Mon–Sat, 9pm–2am*

Ⓔ *Varies, around £6*

Dance

Lakota

6 Upper York Street

(0117) 942 6208

Back in the day, Lakota was a huge sweat-soaked early 90s superclub, and it doesn't seem to have changed much since then. The toilets for one could certainly do with a little spring clean. Legendary psytrance party Tribe of Frog is the friendliest night – a bit of old school UV raver gear will pretty much guarantee you some cuddles from one of the resident hippies. For something a little nastier, big messy mash-ups like Gener8r are a good bet. Get tickets in advance and turn up late or you'll never last 'til 7am.

© *Mon–Thu, 9pm–2am; Fri, 10pm–5am; Sat, 10pm–7am*

€ *£10–£12*

Po Na Na

67 Queens Road

(0117) 904 4445

Like piña coladas and getting caught in the rain? Get souked on cocktails at Moroccan-styled Po Na Na, especially at Tuesday's indie night, Fat Poppadaddy's. Lights are low but effort is cranked up high; despite being a chain, they work to give a twist to proceedings, offering tunage from r 'n' b to live percussion, capoeira and belly dancing, shisha pipes, limos, and laughing gas. It's a key townie draw at weekends, but well worth it for big visiting DJs. Just like the Telly Tubby, a visit to Po will have you demanding 'Again, again!'

© *Mon, Wed & Fri–Sat, 10pm–4am; Tue, 10pm–2.30am; Thu, 10pm–2am*

€ *£2–£7*

Oceana

The South Building, Canons Road

(0117) 927 9203

Whatever you think of Oceana, there's no denying it's big. And we mean bloody big. This superclub has no less than six themed rooms, ranging from an Alpen Ski Lodge (think squelchy sofas and fake moose heads on the walls) to the New York Disco, where the neon light-up dancefloor is perfectly suited to a 70s-stylee dance-off that would see John Travolta going all misty-eyed. Last time Itchy went here we ended up grooving to Phil Collins tunes on said dancefloor. We never claimed to be classy.

© *Mon–Thu, 7.30pm–2.30am; Fri–Sat, 7pm–3.30am*

€ *Free–£4*

Thekla

East Mud Dock, The Grove

(0117) 929 3301

Arrrrr, me hearties, walk the plank, swab the decks, shiver me timbers and dance like there's no tomorrow. No, Itchy hasn't had a stroke, we've just been spending too much time at Thekla, Bristol's very own club-on-a-ship. This two floor venue with stage often plays host to live music, and is particularly good on a Thursday when it's home to Stutter, an indie/alt extravaganza. Always a popular venue, don't be surprised if you find yourself queuing to jump aboard. And if the pirate jokes start to wear a bit thin, why not dust off your *In The Navy* routine to keep those laughs coming?

© *Thu–Sat, 10pm–2am*

€ *£4–£7*

HEN PARTIES
Distinguishing features: Normally perform their all-female pre-mating ritual in a circular dance around sequined receptacles containing grooming apparel. The leader usually wears a letter L and some kind of sexual apparatus on her head.

Survival: For males under 60, camouflage is the best bet. Itchy recommends a bright pink mini-skirt, padded boob tube and red lippy.

HOMO NARCOTICUS
Distinguishing features: This unusual subspecies is mesmerised by repetitive rhythms and flashing lights, and has a peculiar ability to move all limbs and appendages at once in contrary directions, including eyes and ears.

Survival: These malcos are guaranteed to spill their drink on themselves. Put your bev in a bike bottle or go the whole way and throw a sacrificial pint at them before you start dancing.

Safe
Illustration by Thomas Denbigh

and sound

THE DANCE-FLOOR IS A SCARY REALM. IF YOU WANT TO MAKE IT OUT ALIVE, YOU'LL NEED SOME INSIDER KNOWLEDGE, SO GRAB PITH HELMET AND GLO-STICKS AND FOLLOW ITCHY ON A DISCO SAFARI

THE LADS
Distinguishing features: Alpha males indulging in competitive play, such as mixing several beverages in the same glass, and then drinking the whole lot as quickly as possible.

Survival: A propensity to punch the air during power ballads can lead to injury among taller adventurers. Itchy suggests you don a helmet and hit the deck if you hear the line 'Oooh baby do you know what that's worth?'.

UNDERAGE DRINKERS
Distinguishing features: Identified by greasy hair, pale skin and vacant eyes, this genus often regurgitate upon themselves, presenting a hazard to bystanders. Females are impervious to cold and wear very little.

Survival: Enlist their natural predators – larger and more primitive hominids called bouncers, who covet the hair of the underage drinkers, being themselves a furless species.

IF YOU'RE AFTER GUILTY PLEASURES, WHY NOT GO FOR THE OLD CLASSICS? NO, NOT PROSTITUTION AND PICKING YOUR SCABS, BUT CHOCOLATE AND 80S CHEESE

First stop: **Bar Chocolat** (19 The Mall, Clifton, 0117 974 7000). Spend forever choosing between hot chocolate and cake and end up feeling sick after opting for both. Work off the calorie-fest with a brisk walk to Bristol's most exclusive (and expensive) boutiques on **Park Row**. Get out the credit card and buy an extra-special outfit for the meeting with your angry bank manager.

Now it's time for a liquid lunch. Try luxurious **Browns** (9 Perry Road, 0117 330 8445) for scrumptious cocktails, then unwind from the stress of your thus-far shameful behaviour at a spa session in the **Marriott Royal** hotel (College Green, 0117 925 5100) hotel. Again, the bank manager's not going to like it, but you've had three martinis for lunch, so what do you care? Now you're looking like a superstar, it's time to strut your stuff. For the ultimate in guilty pleasures get down to **Reflex** (18a Baldwin Street, 0117 945 8891), the cheesiest, nastiest 80s club ever. Go on, you'll have a ball.

Guilty
pleasures

Illustration by Si Clark
www.si-clark.co.uk

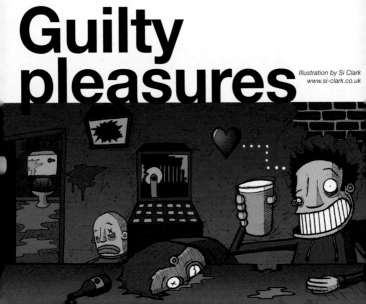

Gay

Gay

BARS

The Pineapple
37 St George Street
(0117) 907 1162

Billing itself as 'Bristol's busiest gay bar', The Pineapple is conveniently close to Vibes and the Queenshilling, making it the perfect pre-clubbing boozer. There's a warm and friendly atmosphere, welcoming staff, and a dancefloor that's ideal for a warm-up prior to some serious stuff-strutting later on, but if it's a quiet night you're after, there's a free quiz on a Tuesday. The Pineapple is also well-known on Bristol's gay scene thanks to the massively popular annual August street party it hosts.

© *Mon–Sat, 1pm–11pm; Sun, 1pm–10.30pm*

CLUBS

Queenshilling
9 Frogmore Street
(0117) 926 4342

If Itchy had a shilling for every time we'd had a rip roaring time here, we'd have amassed a fortune in frustratingly non-spendable currency. Constantly coughs up a fabulous night, and there's no short changing when it comes to the 'queen' part; Queenshilling is Bristol gay royalty, camping it up more than the Brownies on a wilderness weekend. There are no inflated drinks prices; only the music (and buff clientele) are pumped up. We'd give it a crown, but the Shilling is worth even more.

© *Wed, Sun, 10pm–2am; Thu–Sat, 9pm–3am (1st Sat every month, 9pm–6am)*

£ *Free–£5*

PUBS

Old Market Tavern
29–30 Old Market Street
(0117) 922 6123

This gay-friendly local pub specialises in good food and real ale. There's a daily range of lunchtime specials and lots of choice for veggies. The beer garden's great if it's sunny, and if not, there's always the conservatory. Watch out for the OMT melts – a half baguette stuffed with your choice of filling, smothered in cheese and oven-baked. The only problem is that they ain't easy to eat sexily, so it's best consumed when there's only munters in.

© *Mon–Tue, 11.30am–3pm; Wed–Thu, 11.30am–3pm & 7pm–11pm; Fri, 11.30am–11pm; Sat, 7pm–11pm; Sun, 12pm–4pm*

⊕ *OMT melt, £3.75*

Vibes

3 Frog Lane, Frogmore Street
(0117) 934 9076

Located on Frogmore Street, Bristol's equivalent of Manchester's Canal Street (ie, there are all of two gay clubs there), Vibes is a bigger, rowdier counterpart neighbour to The Queenshilling. With two bars and two dancefloors, it's a cavernous club that offers a varied roster of nights. It really can't compete with Wonky, though they come close with Rebellion on Mondays, helmed by DJ Dolly and Miss Treacle Tart: if camp is what you like, you'll fit right in.

🕐 *Mon, 8.30pm–2am; Tue, 10pm–2am;*
Wed, closed; Thu, 10.30pm–3am;
Fri-Sat, 10pm–3am;
💷 *Mon, £2; Tue, £2; Thu, £2/£1 NUS;*
Fri, £4; Sat, £4

SHOPS

Laughter Promotions

www.laughterpromotions.com
(0117) 941 5836

Jumping Jack Flash, it's a gas, gas, gas. Well, no matter who you're jumping, these guys can take the experience to a higher level with laughing gas and more: herbal aphrodisiacs, party poppers, legal pills and thrills, and psychedelics that Itchy, of course, wouldn't know Jack about. If you're hoping to score on a night out but worried about your ball control, their natural performance-enhancing supplements can help you with your keepy-uppies. Hit the back of the net at their web store, and enter ITCHY1 at the checkout to get 10% off.

Wonky at Manhattan Bar

St Nicholas Street
(07763) 723 454

This excellent gay club night might only actually take place once a month but is well worth the wait. Playing an outstanding mix of indie and alternative music that you'll spend all night dancing to, if things got any cooler we'd all die of pneumonia. Also welcoming to straight-types with great taste in music, it attracts a good number of the student gay crowd: think lots of lithe young hotties, getting themselves all sweaty on a packed dancefloor. It may be Wonky, but it certainly ain't broke, and there's no better way to get your fix.

🕐 *Last Friday of every month, 8pm–3am*
💷 *£3*

Gay

OTHER

The Cottage – Bristol's Gay Male Sauna

27–31 West Street, Old Market

(0117) 903 0622

Ah, it's a witty one who named this sweatbox – Itchy sees what they've gone and done. If you've hit all the gay clubs in Bristol and you still haven't pulled then there's always the Cottage Sauna. Slap bang in the centre of Bristol's main gay area, it has a café, sauna, steam room, Jacuzzi, cinema lounge, T.V. lounge, showers and a dark room. And if that's not enough, there's always the intriguing sounding 'fantasy area'...

🕑 *Mon–Thu, 1pm–12am; 24-hour opening at the weekend*

Woodstock Guest House

534 Bath Road, Brislington

(0117) 987 1613

Although sadly not named after the festival (it's the house's original name, dating back to the 1800s), Woodstock is Bristol's only gay-friendly bed and breakfast. Only a mile or so from the town centre, all rooms are en-suite and complete with colour T.V. The entire place is non-smoking, and there's also off-site parking. What really makes it though, is the fabulous garden, which guests are welcome to wander around. Vegetarians are also catered for. They're pretty Inclusive here, you see. Unless of course you're a smoker, but then again it's rare for smokers to be treated like people nowadays.

💷 *Single rooms from £35; doubles from £55*

SO YOU'RE A FRIEND OF DOROTHY WHO'S FOUND THEMSELVES IN A NEW TOWN, AND IT MIGHT AS WELL BE THE EMERALD CITY, YOU'RE SO CLUELESSLY GREEN. HOW DO YOU TRACK DOWN THE BEST PINK PLACES? LET ITCHY GUIDE YOUR RUBY SHOES WITH SOME PEARLS OF WISDOM…

Even if their tastes aren't quite yours, they can give you the lowdown on the more subtle gay haunts, and you and Toto will be going loco in no time.

Scally or pally? – Various gay fetishes for chav-style fashions can make

Gay abandoned

There's no place like homo – Just because you're out of the closet doesn't necessarily mean that you love the great outdoors; camping it up isn't for everyone. However, the most kitsch, flamboyant venues are generally well advertised and typically the easiest ones to find; their mass appeal means you usually get a fair old proportion of straights in there too, enjoying their recommended weekly allowance of cheese, but you should have no trouble tracking down a few native chatty scenesters.

it hard to tell a friendly bear pit from a threatening lions' den full of scallies, especially if you've only heard rumours that somewhere is a non-hetters' hot spot. Be cautious in places packed with trackies unless you want your Adid-ass kicked.

Get board – Internet message boards have honest, frequently updated tips; magazines like *Diva* and *Gay Times* have links to local forums on their sites. Click your mouse, not your heels, and get ready to go on a bender.

Illustration by Si Clark
www.si-clark.co.uk

Shop

Shop

AREAS

Broadmead

Over the years Itchy hasn't been alone in wishing for someone to come along and comprehensively flatten Broadmead (preferably a giant Swedish chef with a fish slice). The place was an eyesore. A weeping pustule on the arse of Bristol. Even worse, it was the first thing to greet most visitors as they entered the city. So when someone finally saw sense and demolished the joint, Itchy rejoiced. It's going to take a while, but once Broadmead has been rebuilt you can expect such wonders as Harvey Nic's, a new House of Fraser and a pack of chav-eating dogs all under the kind of roof Willy Wonka could only dream of. Should all be ready in 2008.

MARKETS

The Slow Food Market
Corn Street

As if you hadn't already guessed, this is a reaction to 'fast food'. The point here is to sell only locally produced and sourced goods of the highest quality. So expect cheeses from Chepstow, bacon from Bristol, scrumpy from Somerset and eggs from a chicken's front bum. There are a few notable exceptions in the form of the bloke selling imported French products such as foie gras, but as he does it with aplomb we'll let him off. The Slow Food Market is on the first Sunday of every month and is more than worth your time. Especially for the eggs.

First Sunday of every month

Park Street

In the absence of any 6000m peaks in the city, many budding mountaineers like to get into shape by simply walking up and down the steep incline of Park Street. We're not joking either. It's commonplace to see cyclists overtaking the cars, completely out of control, screaming for their lives before they slap into the side of the cathedral and perish. But don't let that put you off. For here, among the struggling commuters heaving themselves up Bristol's flanks you'll find an endless array of the finest in fashion, from the magnificent BS8 and Westworld (thankfully not the swaggering moron who'll pimp your ride) to the shoe Meccas of the Boot Room and Cara. The best part is that you'll have buns of steel after a shopping trip here.

St Nicholas Market
Corn Street
(0117) 922 4014

Here, under cover of several roofs you'll find all manner of bric-a-brac, including clothes, books, records, jewellery, a bike shop, the inevitable store selling Naf-Naf and Dreddy trousers and a bunch of people hawking used VHS cassettes. While this is enough to get most people into a tizzy, St Nic's still has an ace; namely the food hall, or the 'sausage man' as he's affectionately known. For a few of your finest pounds the sausage man will provide you with a selection of sausages, some mash, gravy and a fork and will show you somewhere to sit and moan in ecstasy as you stuff yourself. St Nic's also has a curry dude; lunch breaks have never been so good.

DEPARTMENT STORES

House Of Fraser and John Lewis

House Of Fraser – The Horsefair, Broadmead
(0870) 160 7228
John Lewis – The Mall at Cribbs Causeway
(0117) 959 1100

Bristol only has two department stores worth noting: House Of Fraser and John Lewis. If you're so bone idle that you want everything under one roof, then either of these will do you just fine. We're off to one of the other shops listed here to support the local economy.

© *House Of Fraser, Mon–Wed, 9.30am–6pm; Thu, 9am–8pm; Fri, 9.30am–7pm; Sat, 9am–7pm; Sun, 11am–5pm; John Lewis, Mon–Fri, 10am–8pm; Sat, 9am–7pm; Sun, 11am–5pm*

MEN'S CLOTHING

Jack Wills

65 Queens Road
(0117) 922 5854

Are you a student at the University of Bristol? Do you want to look like one? Then shop here. At Jack Wills you'll find everything you need to blend seamlessly into the throng on the Triangle, the hordes on Gloucester Road or the mob on Whiteladies Road. They have pants, trousers, jumpers and, if you ask them nicely, they may even lend you a traffic cone. These guys are so unwaveringly dedicated to the student that the website even mentions exams and coursework. Eek.

© *Mon–Fri, 9.30am–6pm; Sat, 9am–6pm; Sun, 11am–5pm*

Speak easy

HOW TO CHAT LIKE A LOCAL...

If someone hollers 'alright my luvver' as you walk past, don't panic, it's no proposition. Far from wanting to take you as a lover, this is a friendly local greeting. If you hear 'gert lush' on the other hand, you've pulled – someone thinks you're an extreme hottie. Much the same for 'how bist me babber?' – the West Country equivalent of a sexily drawled 'how you doin'?' You might also hear 'ark at ee' (look at you), but reply with a friendly 'ow be' (how are you) and you'll be ok. Alternatively, mutter 'whateverrr, am I bovvered?' à la Vicky Pollard and they'll soon leave you alone. However, we don't advise mockery of the Bristol accent, les you find yourself having to 'coopie down' (crouch) to avoid hurled missiles. NB 'Piss off yon young 'un' is never a good sign.

Shop

UNISEX CLOTHING

BS8

34 Park Street
(0117) 930 4836

Still the best independent clothing retailer in the city. BS8 boasts a staggering array of just about everything for your consumption, all laid out over three floors. Within its hallowed halls you'll find every style currently doing the rounds mixed with enough quirky strangeness to make that oh-so important, distinctive impact that is the difference between being fashion dynamite, and Napoleon Dynamite (although that said Itchy still desperately wants that T-shirt he has with the helicopter on it). Sod Perdo, vote BS8.

☻ *Mon–Sat, 10am–6pm*

Maze

26–28 The Mall, Clifton
(0117) 974 4459

Oh dear Christ, now we're in trouble. Maze is a thoroughly crucifying experience on so many tear-inducing levels. The staff are so jaw-droppingly gorgeous you could hang them on the wall and just look at them all day – they'd let you too, they're so bloody nice. Then there are the clothes; Farhi to Great Plains and absolutely bang up to the minute; so much so that even the coat hangers look cool. There's the price too – despite the fact that Maze is always having a sale of some sort, you're still looking at the better part of sixteen squillion pounds just for one sock. The other one is extra, but oh, that sock…

☻ *Mon–Sat, 9.30am–6pm; Sun, 11am–5pm*

WOMEN'S CLOTHING

Cara

17 Regent Street
(0117) 925 7495

Shoes, shoes and more shoes. Oh, and clothes. Yes, Cara's main focus is on courts, boots and strappy sandals, but, like the clever ducks they are, they've decided to stock some clobber to fit in with the style of shoes they peddle. Classic and elegant, this place manages to stay hip and trendy whilst maintaining its own vibe. From workaday wear to heady heels, you'll find something you can't live without in this store. As Gomez Addams was wont to say to his Morticia, 'Cara mia.'

☻ *Mon–Sat, 10am–6pm; Sun, 12pm–5pm*

DNA

24 Park Street

(0117) 934 9173

Just when you think that nothing fits, every shop is too expensive and you'd rather just go home, curl up on the sofa with some white chocolate and too much white wine, and never go out again because your wardrobe is so unbelievably shit, along comes DNA. This is a place with something for absolutely every girl in the world ever. Well, maybe that's going a little over the top, but we challenge you to wander casually in and leave empty handed – it just ain't possible. DNA is especially good for staple jeans and funky looking tops all costing about the same as a penny chew (after hefty inflation).

🕒 *Mon–Sat, 10am–6pm; Sun, 12pm–5pm*

Uncle Sam's Vintage Clothing

54 Park Street

(0117) 929 8404

An unlikely little second-hand shop that seems to deal solely in dressing a small sub-section of society who want to look like Suede in the early 90s. In many ways of course this is no bad thing, however, if you're in here looking for a particularly nasty woollen-shirt-and-tie combo for a bad taste party, then you're probably in the wrong shop, quite apart from being startlingly unoriginal. These days a bad taste party involves dressing in a way that almost guarantees a good kicking, but sadly, legal reasons mean Itchy can't print its numerous good ideas on this theme. Feel free to email us for advice though.

🕒 *Mon–Sun, 11am–5.30pm*

SECONDHAND

Billie Jean Clothes

208 Gloucester Road

(0117) 944 5353

Here at Itchy, people are always telling us to be careful of what we do. Our mother always told us 'be careful of who you love, and be careful of what you do, 'cause the lie becomes the truth'. A wise woman, Itchy's mum, so we thought it appropriate to say that while we like a good selection of retro clothes as much as the next person, Billie Jean is not our lover. It's just a shop that claims that we are the one. But the kid is not our son. Although we're happy to claim any clothes they may wish to hold us responsible for producing.

🕒 *Mon–Sat, 9.30am–5.30pm*

SHOES

The Boot Room

22 Park Street

(0117) 922 5455

Yet another retail establishment on Park Street; well, we did tell you it is the place to shop. The Boot Room is not, as its name might suggest, a place for sweaty men to leave their football boots before a session of 'see who can pee the highest' in the urinals after a long 90 minutes chasing a bladder around a field. Oh no, here is a refreshing place for those who aren't made of money to find the shoes of their dreams. Now far be it for Itchy to suggest that dreaming of shoes is a bad thing, but if you do, get help. Now.

🕒 *Mon–Sat, 10am–5.45pm*

Shop

BOOKS

Blackwell's
89 Park Street
(0117) 925 1854
Books and then some. You'll feel clever even if you're just buying Jordan's novel.
🕒 *Mon–Fri, 9.30am–7pm; Sat, 9am–7pm; Sun, 11.30am–5.30pm*

Borders
48 Queens Road
(0117) 922 6959
If you're looking for a book in Brizzle, we'll probably see you here, 'cos you just can't keep a good Borders down. This place is open late so you can get your fix of the 20Q game whenever you like.
🕒 *Mon–Sat, 9am–9pm; Sun,12pm–6pm*

Oxfam
26 Princess Victoria Street
(0117) 946 7926
Ever wondered what the danglies Oxfam's name actually means? We wonder if it's the animal equivalent of having a street fam in hip-hop. Then again, quite what having a group of oxen that have always got yo' back when the gats are blazing in the mean streets of Brizzle has to do with ropey second-hand clothing and musty board games, we're not sure. Either way, they do some nice books in this place. Maybe if you got a bible, you could keep it next to your heart to save you from bullet wounds, thus negating the need for a protective herd of bison.
🕒 *Mon–Sat, 9.30am–4.30pm; Sun, 12pm–4.30pm*

Waterstone's
11a The Galleries
(0117) 925 2274
There's something about a shop with more than one floor that just screams 'quality'. You don't see many Woolworths with a floor-guide and an elevator now, do you?
🕒 *Mon–Tue & Fri–Sat, 9am–6pm; Wed, 10am–6pm; Thu, 9am–7pm; Sun, 11am–5pm*

WH Smith
The Galleries
(0117) 925 2152
Is it a stationer? Is it a newsagent? Is it a bookshop? Is it a sweetshop? It's whatever you want it to be, so buy some wine gums and Mills & Boon and stop asking questions.
🕒 *Mon–Wed & Fri–Sat, 8.30am–5.30pm; Thu, 8.30am–7pm; Sun, 11am–5pm*

MUSIC

And the Beat Goes On
24 Cotham Hill

This is exactly what the world would look like if all the money guzzling, faceless, giant, inhumane record stores were eaten by an enormous ferret called Ron. Here you'll find new and used vinyl, cassettes, VHS, DVD, books and some weird things we couldn't recognise. The owner's sole intent is to be a nice bloke; and he doesn't appear interested in turning you upside down and shaking you until all of your money falls from your pockets. He's not a spotty idiot with half a GCSE in being obnoxious either.
📞 *Open from whenever the door is open until whenever it's closed*

HMV
21–23 Broadmead
(0117) 929 7647

Hum Music Vocally. That's what we believe the initials 'HMV' stand for, and we like to obey this instruction to the letter when stood plugged in to the listening posts.
📞 *Mon, Wed–Sat, 9am–6pm; Tue, 9.30am–6pm; Sun, 11am–5pm*

Virgin Megastore
The Galleries
(0117) 929 7798

Don't feel like a corporate whore shopping here. There are days when all you want to do is froth at the mouth in a consumerist haze while you spend, spend, spend.
📞 *Mon–Wed & Fri–Sat, 9am–6pm; Thu, 9am–7pm; Sun, 11am–5pm*

Fopp
43 Park Street
(0117) 945 0685

Fopp is a particularly virulent menace. Fopp is the kind of store that haunts your dreams, making you want things you've never heard of, and entices you to its seductively-stacked shelves like the queen of all sirens. Fopp is, without a shadow of a doubt, responsible for 18.9% of all credit card debt in Bristol (and did you ever hear that 87.2% of statistics are made up on the spot?). You'll be offered music, DVDs, books and culture at prices to boggle modern maths. You'll be made to feel like the entire back catalogue of *The Prisoner* is a must-have. This place WILL make you poor. But how we love it.
📞 *Mon–Sat, 9am–6pm; Sun, 11am–6pm*

FOOD

Kin Yip Hon Chinese Supermarket
16a St Thomas Street
(0117) 929 9098

A veritable treasure trove of goodies, this is one supermarket where you won't have some numb-nuts sounding like Sloth from *The Goonies* asking if you want 'cash back'. Hidden away in a part of town that seems, architecturally, to be recovering from a war that no one else noticed, is this absolute gem. Step inside and experience the kind of awed wonder you had when you were a kid and it started snowing outside. And it's all so very cheap. Ditch your local super-rip-off and come here.
📞 *Mon–Sun, 10am–6pm*

Shop

The Organic Supermarket
The Proving House, Sevier Street, St Werburghs
(0117) 935 1725

Organic stuff is everywhere these days; you can get organic flip-flops, organic mobile phones – even organic pets. So why would you drive all the way to a lousy part of town to get your organic stuff? We'll tell you why; it's because these folks mean it. A lot. Here everything is organic, no messing about. Everything. You can even make a saving on some of your 'normal' environment-murdering stuff. Bring your own tubs and things like muesli, flour, couscous and rice are all available loose, saving you a great deal of cash, and saving a little bit of your planet at the same time.

☻ *Mon–Wed, 9am–6pm; Thu–Fri, 9am–7pm; Sat, 9am–5pm*

Gash
www.gash.co.uk

When Itchy's mate Dave discovered this über-classy online erotic emporium, stocking lingerie, cosmetics, books, lotions, and lady-pleasing toys including the 'Tongue Joy', he declared, 'That's just like the rhyming kitchen product; Gash – loves the jobs you hate'. This revealed both his dire bedroom prowess and an acute lack of grease-busting knowledge – that's Mr Muscle, not Flash, twazzock. When he's finished with the sink, we've got his girlie some personalised pants to help him patch things up, with a photo of his mug and the words 'Dave, come on down'. Our own deluxe satin pair look stunning, but maybe having them embroidered with 'Itchy' wasn't such a good idea.

OTHER

Corks of Cotham
54 Cotham Hill
(0117) 973 1620

Here at Itchy we like to think we know a little bit about wine – for the most part that starts at which end to pour from and finishes with us asking if it comes with a straw. If like us, every now and again you find yourself in need of a little help, Corks is just the place. We can all get a two-for-one deal down the local corner shop, but when you need to impress someone, not just render them unconscious, you could do a lot worse. Here the staff actually know stuff about wine; like what each colour tastes like, and where it comes from. Amazing.

☻ *Mon–Sat, 10am–9pm*

Workshop
1–2 Perry Road
(0117) 922 1566

Itchy was brought up to believe that all workshops are necessarily stocked by elves. We're not sure where this place sourced their funky little dudes, but they've royally trumped any midget workforce Father Christmas or Willy Wonka could come up with. Their teeny hands create everything from limited edition trainers and badges featuring worldwide graffiti to eye-magnet design books and miniature robots. They've even crafted an exhibition space for local artists, resulting in a shop with real personality and more edginess than a dodecahedron. A small wonder.

☻ *Mon–Sat, 10am–5.30pm; Sun, 11am–4pm*

IF YOU THINK VEGGIES ARE CRANKY, YOU'LL LOVE THIS. FREEGANS SAY OUR ECONOMIC SYSTEM HURTS THE ENVIRONMENT, TREATS ANIMALS CRUELLY AND WORKERS UNFAIRLY, AND WASTES RESOURCES, SO YOU SHOULDN'T PAY FOR FOOD. IDIOTS. HERE'S HOW WE'D BE FREEGANS…

1. Have a Pret dinner – The bods who run Pret a Manger obviously don't know much about the principles of Freeganism, given how much they throw away each day. Turn up at closing, rummage through their bin bags, and hey presto – free dinner.

2. Kill an animal – Apparently it's legal for you to kill squirrels on your own property. With this in mind, set up a bird table, cover it in superglue and get the pot boiling while you wait for it to become a squirrel lolly. Sure, you might snare the odd bird, but extra protein's always welcome, and the RSPB'll never catch you.

3. Forage – Those in the country could nick apples from trees and scour woodland floors for wild mushrooms. Alternatively, those of us whose parents aren't blood-related to each other could pull half-eaten trays of late-night chips from bins.

4. Mug a milkman – Those bastards don't need all that milk. But you do. Being a freegan isn't conducive to a calcium-rich diet, after all. Wait until your local milky's delivering to a dark area, then knock him out and chug as many bottles as you can before making your getaway.

5. Sniper rifle the zoo – Get up high, and train your gun on the elephant cage. It's not going to be easy to take one of those suckers down with one shot, but if it pays off, you'll be eating like a monarch for weeks. Plus you could sell the tusks on to practitioners of Chinese medicine for extra cash.

Freegan fun

Illustration by Thomas Denbigh

0800700200
FREE
PHONE

G.A.N
SKIP HIRE

Out & about

Out & about

CINEMAS

The Cube
4 Princess Row
(0117) 907 4190

This TARDIS-like microplex seems small from the outside, but is packed with more strange geographical goings-on than you can shake a Dalek at. A home from home for oddball arty types, its programme is diverse, with new film releases cosying up alongside low-budget indie productions and live events. While you're there why not sample some Cube-Cola at the bar, home-made from a recipe found on a website, for a taste of anti-commercialism. Or just go to Woolworths and pick up a bottle of Coke on your way there.
🅐 £2–£5

The Watershed
1 Canons Wharf
(0117) 927 5100

The Watershed has everything you could want from an arthouse cinema: a lineup that always features the very finest in cutting-edge indie and non-mainstream filmmaking, with a special focus on contemporary European cinema; comfy seats since the extensive refurb; a (packed) bar that serves great food, especially the nachos. And they don't sell popcorn so no bastard can ruin your film by snaffling away like a pig and throwing bits of it at his girlfriend in presumably what passes for foreplay in some circles. Talk during the film and die: this is the way it should be.
🅐 £3.50 before 5pm; after 5pm, adults, £6, concs £4

Odeon
Union Street
(0871) 224 4007

Mighty and established king of the cinema clones since the year dot, the Odeon Broadmead is like every other Odeon you've ever been to. If anything it's perhaps a little bit smaller and more weirdly laid out than the usual, but the popcorn and drinks are still uniformly extortionate. The limited number of screens usually means that only the most mainstream fare is on offer, but sometimes that's just the cinematic fix you need. And if you're fancying watching something a teensy bit more highbrow, The Watershed is only a short walk away. Also on the plus side, students get a good discount.
🅐 £5.20; students, £4.20

COMEDY CLUBS

Jesters Comedy Club
142 Cheltenham Road
(0117) 909 6655

This place bills itself as 'pant-wettingly funny' – whether this is a good thing is not for us to decide. They do, however, insist that on their 'stand-up and boogie' nights (performance followed by disco) all the comedians that appear have gigged at the Comedy Store London, so the standard's pretty good. Thursdays are Meal Deal nights – 3 comedians and grub for a tenner – and Wednesday is student night.
🄾 Doors, 7.30pm for 9pm
🅐 Wed, student night, £5 NUS; Thu, Meal Deal, £10 for meal and performance; Sat, Stand–up and Boogie, £12

Out & about

THEATRES

Alma Tavern
18–20 Alma Vale Road, Clifton
(0117) 973 5171

'A theatre in a pub, you say?' Yes, we certainly do say. This tiny, 50 seat palace of entertainment is above the Alma Tavern pub and puts on productions by local company Theatre West. There's something deeply wholesome about the whole affair. They let you take a drink in to the performances, and the pub does some great food (better than your average pub grub) if the strain on your heart strings of so much culture leaves you feeling a bit peckish. Productions tend to be pretty good – anything really dire and there's always the option of sneaking back out to the bar.

Bristol Old Vic
King Street
(0117) 987 7877

Located in a particularly attractive part of central Bristol, this place is a legend in thesp circles. The Old Vic shows a bit of everything from intellectual productions of Victorian classics to new writing and minimalist Shakespeare. Pay-what-you-can nights for main house performances mean you can see a decent play for just £3.50, even though you might end up behind a pillar or squashed up with your knees around your ears and an old lady practically sitting on your lap furiously sucking mint humbugs. Suffering for the sake of art and all that. But usually you suffer for your own art, not someone else's.
🎭 £3.50–£24.50

The Bristol Hippodrome
St Augustine's Parade, City Centre
(0117) 926 5524

The menu at this big, shiny place at the bottom of Park Street is jolly but predictable. The usual suspects appear in the form of polished West End musicals, and the annual pantomime with some additional glitter in the form of one or more minor TV celebrities. Over the past few years, 2005's tale of love and valour saw Dave Benson-Phillips (you remember, the bloke from *Get Your Own Back*... what? You don't recall?) and Julian Clary camping it up in *Cinderella*, and 2006's *Peter Pan* featured 'Joe of the Jungle' Pasquale as a helium-voiced Bosun Smee. But enough of the snobbery – this is classic entertainment.
🎭 £11.50–£25.50

Out & about

The Old Tobacco Factory
Raleigh Road, Southville
(0117) 902 0344

Housed inside the former Wills Tobacco Factory, this place avoided all ambiguity in the naming process – if you're lucky you might catch the odd hammered punter scratting in the corners in search of a crumbly old ciggie when their own supply runs dry. Fortunately they're a little more adventurous when it comes to putting on productions, which range from blood and guts Shakespearean extravaganzas in the form of the gruesome *Titus Andronicus*, to postmodernist performance art. They play host to touring companies, have an annual Christmas family show, and put on two Shakespeare plays every summer.
✪ Prices vary

The Architecture Centre
Narrow Quay
(0117) 922 1540

You'd expect the name of this place to be pretty self explanatory but oh no, no, no, no, no, no, no. The Architecture Centre is about so much more than the art of building stuff. Obviously, there are a number of architecture exhibitions or they'd be guilty of some form of deeply devious false advertising, but alongside these they also feature the work of designers, public artists, jewellers – all sorts really. Their exhibitions change regularly, making this one of the country's top architecture galleries outside London. And if you've got the cash then the gift shop's pretty cool, too.
☀ Tue–Fri, 11am–5pm;
Sat–Sun, 12pm–5pm

The QEH Theatre
Berkely Place, Berkely
(0117) 930 3044

Nothing to do with an opulent if troubled cruise ship named after the old dear over in Buckingham Palace, this theatre is essentially the art and drama department for the attached private boys' school. As well as hosting performances put on by the school, the QEH Theatre also welcomes poets, theatre companies, comics, musicians and dancers to come and entertain the masses. Offering everything from the Bard to contemporary poetry, the QEH's varied brochure is bound to have something to appeal. Girls should probably watch out for the sixth form students though. Remember they're much too young for you.

GALLERIES

Arnolfini
16 Narrow Quay, Harbourside
(0117) 917 2305

This contemporary arts space has an ever-changing programme of exhibitions, some beautiful, thought-provoking and intelligent, others something your pet gerbil could have doodled. That said, the good usually outweighs the bad, and there's a truly wonderful bookshop selling a huge variety of art, theatre, film and photography books and a selection of weird and wonderful magazines. The café-bar's very nice for a quick coffee (or cocktail) too.
☀ Gallery, Mon–Wed & Fri–Sun, 10am–8pm;
Thu, 10am–6pm; Café-bar, Mon–Sat,
10am–11pm; Sun, 10am–10.30pm

Royal West of England Academy

Queen's Road

(0117) 973 5129

This is the place for those of you who think modern art's a load of bison crap and that the muppet who paid £74m for a Jackson Pollock painting was ripped off big time. This beautiful building is stuffed full of traditional paintings, including a wide selection of work by British artists. However, it's not just gubbins from centuries ago – there are some contemporary exhibitions, but don't come here looking for unmade beds, pickled sealife or a grown man who dresses like a cross between Andy Pandy and Bette Davis circa *Baby Jane*.

🕒 *Mon–Sat, 10am–5.30pm; Sun, 2pm–5pm*

💷 £3

Spike Island

133 Cumberland Road, Spike Island, Bristol Docks

(0117) 929 2266

No, no, Spike Island isn't a ride at Euro Disney or the next film in *The Pirates of the Caribbean* franchise (but maybe it should be). It's a gallery and creative arts space with real artists' studios giving a genuinely arty aura. It's only recently reopened after a £2.25m refurbishment so is nicely jazzed up, too. They've also come up with a 'design incubator' concept and are providing office space for up-and-coming fashion designers, illustrators and animators. All the cool kids are going to be there – head on down and you never know, maybe someone will discover you as their muse. Maybe.

🕒 *Mon–Sun, 12pm–5pm*

Out & about

MUSEUMS

Bristol City Museum and Art Gallery

Queen's Road, Clifton

(0117) 922 3571

Housed in the magnificent building next to Bristol's Wills Memorial Building and home to a huge range of exhibitions, from fossils and archaeology to Egyptian artefacts, ceramics and modern art. There are new exhibitions popping up all the time making this free (yes, free) attraction essential to anyone who needs to gen up on their history. It's probably worth doing a couple of short visits rather than one great big cultural overload, though, as there's a lot to see.

🕐 *Mon–Sun, 9am–5pm*

💷 *Free*

The Georgian House

7 Great George Street

(0117) 921 1362

This Georgian house (you'd never guess from the name, would you?) is tucked away in a street off Park Street and has been preserved just as it would have been if you'd popped in for a cup of tea and a Bourbon cream (did they have them back then?) during the 18th Century. Formerly the home of prosperous West India merchant John Pinney, the house takes you back to the time when Britain's colonial clout kept the world firmly under its boot heel and the bustling port town of Bristol was busily prospering. Pop down and, by George, you'll be both entertained and well-educated.

🕐 *Sat–Wed, 10am–5pm; Thu & Fri, closed*

The British Empire and Commonwealth Museum

Clock Tower Yard, Temple Meads

(0117) 925 4980

Hop over to Brunel's impressive 19th century Temple Meads railway station, and you're on track for a sombre afternoon. An exploration of Britain when it was a big colonial player and the sun never set on the old British empire, this museum plays particular (and commendable) attention to Bristol's less than glorious past as a key city in the British slave trade. It succeeds in teaching you a lot without boring you to tears and you'll see Whiteladies Road and Blackboy Hill in a completely different light afterwards.

🕐 *Mon–Sun, 10am–5pm*

💷 *£6.95*

LIVE MUSIC

The Bunch of Grapes

8 Denmark Street

(0117) 987 0500

www.thebunchofgrapes.co.uk

Tucked behind the Hippodrome, this was always going to attract creative types. They host a live blues night every Tuesday, live music on a Friday and Saturday, and acoustic sessions on Sundays. Come along to listen, or if you're feeling tuneful, sign up for Wednesday's open-mic night. For those among you who go a little wobbly in the gizzards at the thought of carrying a tune, the beer's good and there's a great jukebox. Press the button and the songs come out – now that's musicianship.

🕐 *Times and prices vary according to event*

Fiddlers Club
Willway Street, Bedminster
(0117) 987 3403

Like the kids at Itchy's school whose surname was Down, and whose parents saw fit to christen them Ben and Neil, this venue's funny title prompts more snorting than when Pete and Kate had Richard Bacon over for tea. In any case, it's packed to the rafters with the cream of live artists (Manu Chao, Nithin Sawhney, Lee Scratch Perry, Magic Numbers, KT Tunstall...), and run by a passionate family team who really know their musical onions. Getting there isn't half as hard as you'd think and the ambiance is twice as good as you could imagine. Licensed until 2am, once you're in, you'll want to fiddlestick around.

Ⓒ *Times and prices vary*

Out & about

Carling Academy

Frogmore Street

(08707) 712 000

Ever wished you could see the bands you know and love with a whole host of similarly-minded young things? Well, boy oh boy; Christmas has come early for you this year and just look what Itchy Claus has in our sack. The Carling Academy is pretty much the only port of call for big bands visiting Bristol, and the lineups are always guaranteed to feature big names with rocking support bands. Everyone from Bloc Party to Basement Jaxx have turned up, so living in Brizzle you'll probably end up here sooner or later.

◉ *Times vary depending on event; doors 7pm unless specified*

🎫 *Ticket prices vary, book in advance*

Fleece & Firkin

12 St Thomas Street

(0117) 945 0996

From hushed awe to bouncing mosh pits of the silliest variety, The Fleece has been home to many a magical musical experience. Probably a lot of extremely average ones as well, but as a gig venue the place does somehow seem to bring out the best in bands. We know people say this about loads of places, but it's a great venue to catch acts on the cusp of fame and, for the more adventurous amongst you, they put on lots of unsigned bands too. If you're a bit brassick then probably best get a beer next door first; the bar's fairly pricey.

◉ *Mon–Thu, 8pm–12am; Fri–Sat, 8pm–1am; Sun, 7.30pm–11pm*

🎫 *£7–£10*

The Prom

26 The Promenade, Gloucester Road

(0117) 942 7319

Sitting outside in Bristol is often a worse idea than going for a swim with Michael Barrymore. Yet when it's balmy, there's no better place to chill with a pint and good grub than The Prom. When it's brisker, they have heaters. And when it's brisker than a cheetah facing the right way in a wind tunnel, they have free wi-fi inside. But what this venue's really about is top quality live music in a range of genres wider than Rick Waller's backside. And the one night of the week they're not rocking the roof? Tuesday, when they hold a cracking pub quiz. This, my friend, is the mutt's nuts. We (ahem) Prom-ise.

🕐 *Times and entry vary*

Let's get physical

Hate the gym? No worries. Check out **Pole Play's** (Top Notch Health Club, The Pithay, All Saints Street, 07900 483 155, £12.50 per person) pole dancing classes. There's no nudity involved, although what you get up to in your own time is your business. If you'd prefer clambering over a cliff face to spinning around a stick, **Undercover Rock** offers 4½ hour beginners' classes to have you wallcrawling with confidence within two weeks. Still don't feel like getting off the sofa? How about a spot of funk dancing? **Funk It Up** hip hop dance school (Funk It Up Dance School, The Coach House, Unit 28, 2 Upper York Street, lessons, £5 per person) is a good bet, with teachers including a bloke who's shown the likes of Britney Spears and Michael Jackson how to shake their booty.

Out & about

SPORT

Bristol City FC
Ashton Gate
(0117) 963 0630

If you go and support the local Coca Cola League 2 side, whatever you do, don't wear blue. No, not even if it's your wedding day. City play in red and white, and supporters would be wise to attire themselves in these colours to avoid being mistaken for a Bristol Rovers fan (which, trust us, is what is commonly known as 'a fate worse than death'). Locals round here are fiercely loyal to their chosen boys, and very vocal in their support – learn a few offensive chants about Bristol's other key team (something about their mums is usually good) and you'll fit right in.

Bristol Ice Rink
John Nike Leisure Sport, Frogmore Street
(0117) 929 2148

In these asbo-ridden times, ice skating seems so beautifully innocent. Even if the world has moved forwards, a little bit of that Disney magic still dwells in the John Nike Leisure Centre (which Ali G didn't save in his film). Smile benevolently at youths who like nothing better than spinning in circles and getting chilly fingers. It's like some sort of ancient courtship ritual; the bigger boys skate really fast in their non-regulation black skates while the girls let their hair blow prettily in the wind as they mouth along to Girls Aloud. The walls are painted with rainbows, *Children's Ward*-style, and the bar pours a fine Breezer. Great fun, irony-free.

Bristol Community Dance Centre
Jacobs Wells Road, Hotwells
(0117) 929 2118

This community dance centre offers a mind-boggling array of boogie classes for everyone, from the most uncoordinated of beginners to those who can even tell their left foot from their right (Itchy can but dream of this level of prowess on the dance floor). Choose from flamenco, salsa, pan-African dance, Bollywood dance, hip-hop, capoeira, break-dancing, funky dance, contemporary dance – bloody hell, we're feeling dizzy just deciding which class to go to. The centre also holds children's classes and youth classes, as well as offering yoga, pilates, and jitsu lessons.
© *Class times and prices vary*

Bristol Rovers FC
Memorial Stadium, Horfield
(0117) 909 6648

Now we're not going to lie to you – going to watch this league 3 team isn't going to be the sort of poetry in motion you've come to expect from televised Premiership matches, but heck, give them some credit. They're trying like there's no tomorrow, and a lot of the time something a little less polished can be much more exciting anyway. If you decide that these boys are the team for you, wear a vibrant blue, avoid your sworn enemies the Bristol City supporters like the plague, and if you are unfortunate enough to encounter them, kill the bastards on sight. (Disclaimer: Itchy in no way condones football hooliganism or violence of any sort).

Stag & hen

Illustration by Thomas Denbigh

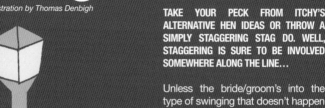

TAKE YOUR PECK FROM ITCHY'S ALTERNATIVE HEN IDEAS OR THROW A SIMPLY STAGGERING STAG DO. WELL, STAGGERING IS SURE TO BE INVOLVED SOMEWHERE ALONG THE LINE...

Unless the bride/groom's into the type of swinging that doesn't happen in park play areas (if it does – hell, you need to move to a better estate), by saying 'I do' your friend is promising not to indulge in bratwurst boxing with anyone but their chosen partner. For £52 per person, you can make sure they pack in the porking prior to the big day at a sausage-making course (www.osneylodgefarm.co.uk), and fry up the results the morning after to calm your hangovers.

As they're already selflessly donating themselves to someone else for life, chuck some extra charity in the mix; if you can raise enough cash for a good cause, experiences like bungee jumping, fire walking and skydiving are absolutely free. Wedding guests could pledge sponsorship as part of their gifts to the couple, and the money saved could go towards an extra few days on the honeymoon. Suitable charities for those getting hitched to munters include the Royal National Institute of the Blind or Battersea Dogs' Home.

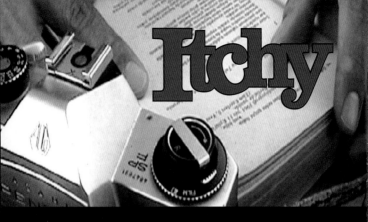

Calling all aspiring scribblers
and snappers...

We need cheeky writers and hawk-eyed photographers to contribute
their sparkling talents to the Itchy city guides and websites.
We want the inside track on the bars, pubs, clubs and restaurants in
your city, as well as longer features and dynamic pictures to represent
the comedy, art, music, theatre, cinema and sport scenes.

If you're interested in getting involved, please send examples of your
writing or photography to: editor@itchymedia.co.uk, clearly stating
which city you can work in. All work will be fully credited.

**Bath/Birmingham/Brighton/Bristol/Cambridge/Cardiff/Edinburgh/
Glasgow/Leeds/Liverpool/London/Manchester/
Nottingham/Oxford/Sheffield/York**

Laters

Laters

Late (or early) energy stop

We've all been there at one stage or another. You're planning to hit the town with your mates tonight, and it's going to be immense, but you just can't seem to keep you eyes open. Never fear, for The Boston Tea Party (75 Park Street, 0117 929 8601) is ready and waiting to wire you to the eyeballs with enough caffeine to keep you twitching for a week, and they'll do it 'til 10pm every Thursday through to Saturday. Even better, Boston T (as Itchy likes to call it) flings open its doors at 7am (except Sunday) to help those of you rocking up as your last stop on a particularly heavy night.

Late drinks

You've had a brilliant night out, but somehow you seem to have lost about three hours in a combination rant about traffic wardens and blokes who wear eyeliner, and now the bar staff are putting the stools on the tables in that very definite 'game over' way. Someone suggests a club, but you have no interest in dancing. You want another drink. Fortunately, help is at hand. Stumble over to All In One (46 Park Street, 0117 926 5622), which, although looking a touch like an Ikea showroom, will welcome more civilised drunkards until 3am on Fridays and Saturdays.

Find yourself on St Michael's aching for another drink? Well, although we find it a bit soulless these days since it went all 'upmarket' – i.e. the ancient beer posters are gone and the ceiling's been painted red – Roxy Café Bar (19–20 Perry Road, 0117 930 4113) is still the best (and in fact only) place around for a bit of chilled late night drinking. Free cheesy garlic bread goes some way towards offering a consolation for the bizarrely expensive bevvies they do here, but like they say, beggars can't be choosers, right?

Think you're a smidge too classy for all that? Maybe The Woods (1 Park Street Avenue, Clifton 0117

925 0890) is more your cup of, well, single malt whiskey we suppose. They boast one of the finest selections in Bristol, but if you don't fancy swirling peaty, smoky-tasting goodness round your mouth, order cocktails 'til 6am at weekends, or for real philistines perhaps a pitcher of Grolsch. What with its leather, wood and strange faunae on the walls, the place has a bit of a gentlemen's club vibe which might not appeal to everyone, but it's best not to nitpick. The sophisticated late-night lounging is worlds above clubbing it up in some sticky-floored sewer as the exposed spare tyres wobble and the white shirt boys put their hands in the air for Abba.

Late music and entertainment

Prefer a little more atmosphere or maybe a bit of nosh to just ragging down the pints like the bar's going to take off any second on a one way trip to Pluto? There is no comparison to Mr Wolf's (33 St Stephen's Street, 0117 927 3221) which combines yummy noodles, live music, and of course, something to quench your thirst. Dedicated lushes can stay until their latest hour of 4am from Wednesdays through to Saturdays, taking in the moody décor and beats. If jazz is more your pleasure, Tantric Jazz Café Bar (39-41 St Nicholas Street, 0117 940 2304) will not disappoint, with nightly

music ranging from mainstream Western to Eastern and Latin jazz, blues, soul, and world music. Reasonably-priced tapas and an alluring candlelit intimacy make it a sure hit, especially since it's open until 3am daily. The Thekla Social (The Grove, East Mud Dock, 0117 929 3301) has had a face lift of late, and we reckon you'll like it. No more coughing up your life savings for two cans of lukewarm Red Stripe and flailing around to reggae in the dark. It's now sporting skinny jeans and a shaggy fringe in its new incarnation as an all-purpose indie/electro hotspot. Check it out for gigs of the quirky guitar-pop variety from their regular bands.

Late Eats

'Fancy a tepid kebab?' suggests your drunken mate. 'Noooooo,' you slur back, 'it's a Ragged Mole for me.' You are, of course, referring to the wrap Mecca that is Magic Roll (3 Queen's Row, Triangle South, Clifton, 0117 922 1435). Itchy is not proud to be able to vouch that their staff are remarkably patient when you stagger in jabbing at the wide range of toppings, yelling 'MAGIC ROLL!' in an infuriating manner. However, they are open until 3am on Thursdays, Fridays and Saturdays, so while you might leave a bit embarrassed, you'll have a hell of a drunk munchie in your hand.

Fun @ night

DON'T WASTE THE GIFT OF INSOMNIA BY COUNTING IMAGINARY ANIMALS – GO CREATE SOME SHEAR (ARF) MAYHEM IN THE EARLY AM AND ENTER THE ITCHY TWILIGHT ZONE. WE WOOL IF YOU WOOL

Go jousting – First up, feed up for some insane-sbury's prices. As witching hours approach, 24-hour supermarkets reduce any unsold fresh produce to mere coppers; pick up a feast for a few pauper's pennies and buy them clean out of 10p French sticks, which are spot on for sword fights. Up the ante by jousting using shopping trolleys or bicycles in place of horses, or start a game of ciabatta-and-ball by bowling a roll.

Play street games – Take some chalk to sketch a marathon hopscotch grid down the entire length of the thoroughfare, or an anaconda-sized snakes and ladders board writhing across your town square. Break the trippy silence and deserted stillness of the dead shopping areas with a tag, catch or British bulldog competition, and be as rowdy as you like – there's no-one around to wake.

Play Texaco bingo – Alternatively, drive the cashier at the all-night petrol station honey nut loopy by playing Texaco bingo: the person who manages to make them go back and forth from the window the most times to fetch increasingly obscure, specific and embarrassing items wins. Along with your prize-winning haul of mango chutney-flavoured condoms, Tena Lady towelettes and tin of eucalyptus travel sweets, be sure to pick up a first-edition paper to trump everyone over toast with your apparently psychic knowledge of the day ahead's events-to-be. Whatever you do, remember: you snooze, you lose.

Illustration by Thomas Denbigh

Book cut-price, last minute accommodation with Itchy Hotels

Itchy Hotels has a late booking database of over 500,000 discount

hotel rooms and up to 70% off thousands of room rates in 4-star and

5-star hotels, bed and breakfasts, guesthouses, apartments and luxury

accommodation in the UK, Ireland, Europe and worldwide.

hotels.itchycity.co.uk

or book by phone: 0870 478 6317

Sleep

SWANKY

Avon Gorge Hotel
Sion Hill
(0117) 973 8955

Look elsewhere if you're not after four-poster chic. However, it is going to mean you missing out on unbeatable views.
🎝 *Singles, from £116; doubles, from £126*

Bristol Marriott Royal Hotel
College Green
(0117) 925 5100

Ooh, it's a bit snazzy this one. Luxury facilities, swimming pool, spa, cocktail bar, swanky restaurant. Staying here will most likely bankrupt you but, my word, you'll have done it in style.
🎝 *Doubles, from £134*

Hotel Du Vin & Bistro
The Sugar House, Narrow Lewins Mead
(0117) 925 5577

A luxury weekend in Bristol doesn't get any better than staying here. The rooms are large and luxurious, the showers feel like heated waterfalls, there's a first class restaurant on your doorstep and the bar comes complete with a proper old-fashioned billiards table. But the best thing here is the way it's all about booze. The wine list in the bar resembles a small phone book, the rooms are named after champagne producers, and the décor makes you feel like you're in a splendidly well-kept wine cellar. We hope that when we die and go to heaven, we'll be able to spend infinity in a place a bit like this.
🎝 *From £130*

☐☐☐☐☐☐☐☐☐▨☐☐

MID-RANGE

The Clifton Hotel
St Paul's Road
(0117) 973 6882

This reasonably priced hotel is just minutes from Clifton village and is fully en suite, so no running down the corridor to take a crap.

Singles, from £65; doubles, from £85

Holiday Inn Express
Temple Gate
(0870) 400 9670

It might not look much cop from the outside, but the location more than makes up for that. Opposite the station, it's an ideal place to stick visitors who you don't want hanging around making your pad look untidy.

From £139

CHEAP

Arches Hotel
132 Cotham Brow
(0117) 924 7398

This family-owned vegetarian hotel has a strict non-smoking policy. Cosy with excellent vegetarian and vegan breakfasts.

Singles, from £28.50; doubles, from £50.50

Toad Lodge
Cotham Park
(0117) 924 7080

This family run hotel in trendy Cotham is a pet-friendly place with a non-smoking policy. It offers en suite rooms and off-road parking but bear in mind it doesn't accept credit or debit cards.

Singles, from £25; doubles, from £35

Victoria Square Hotel
Victoria Square, Clifton
(0117) 973 9058

The rooms are good but on the small side and the dining's adequate. But the location is amazing. Less than 5 minutes from the centre of Clifton Village, the hotel is on Victoria Square, a lovely little patch of green.

Singles, from £59; doubles, from £75

Washington Hotel
St Paul's Road
(0117) 973 3980

This cosy hotel offers a full English breakfast, private parking and satellite T.V. Some rooms are en suite, others three to a bathroom. There's no restaurant but you're not far from the eating establishments of Clifton.

Singles, from £48; doubles, from £77

White House Guest Rooms
28 Dean Lane
(0117) 953 7725

This family-run guest house is located just half a mile from the city centre. It has 15 cosy rooms and offers a complimentary breakfast of cereal and toast. There's also a nice terrace area and plenty of off-road parking.

Singles, from £25; doubles, from £46

YHA
14 Narrow Quay
(0870) 770 5726

This good-quality youth hostel is bang in the middle of the vibrant waterfront area. It also has laundry facilities, complimentary breakfast, internet access and a T.V. lounge. Parking nearby is pricey.

From £19.95

Useful info

Useful info

HAIRDRESSERS

Nikita Hair
67 Broadmead
(0117) 922 0680
Ever wondered what Nikita did after killing all those baddies? Err, no, neither do we.

Reflections
131 Whiteladies Road
(0117) 973 8718
Never wear a hat. Only a smile. And clothes.

BEAUTY SALONS

Wish
22–24 Gloucester Road, Bishopston
(0117) 907 7446
Cross your fugly fingers they'll do their best.

TATTOO AND PIERCING

The Tattoo Studio
232 Cheltenham Road
(0117) 907 7407
More needles than a Christmas tree.

Holy Skin
367 Bat Road
(0117) 907 6567
Experts at sticking metal through people.

OTHER

The Red Flower Barrow Florist
24a Gloucester Road, Bishopston
(0117) 942 0052

Regent Pharmacy
13 Regent Street, Clifton
(0117) 973 5500

Smart Talk
88a Park Street
(0117) 930 4304
If you're immobile without your mobile, and it may as well be called a brain-cell phone because you can't think without it, try this lot. They offer repairs, parts, accessories and unlocking on pretty much all models, and pay cash for damaged handsets, so if your Samsung's stopped singing, your Motorola-coaster's come off the tracks, your LG's D.O.A. or your Nokia's saying 'No', pay Smart Talk a visit. They also cut keys, refill and replace printer cartridges, and repair PCs and laptops, including spyware removal.

CAR HIRE

Avis Rent a Car
Rupert Street
(0870) 608 6325

TAXIS

Bristol and Avon Taxis
36a Gloucester Road, Bishopston
(0117) 942 0000

Swiftline Taxis
181a Hotwells Road, Hotwells
(0117) 925 2626

Yellow Cab Co
36 Bedminster Parade
(0117) 923 1515

TRAINS

Bristol Temple Meads Train Station
(0845) 700 0125
Only 10 minutes from the city centre.

Bristol Parkway Train Station
(0845) 700 0125
Four bloody miles from the city centre.

First Great Western
(08457) 000 125
www.firstgreatwestern.co.uk

PLANES

Bristol Airport
(0870) 121 2742

FISH AND CHIPS

Clifton Village Fish Bar
1 Princess Victoria Street
(0117) 974 1894
Excellent selection of fish and seafood.

Rendezvous
9 Denmark Street
(0117) 929 8683
Voulez-vous? With these chips? Mais oui!

FALAFEL

Falafel King
City Centre, near The Waterfront
(0785) 571 5676
Scrummy, fresh falafel, salads and sauces.

ORIENTAL TAKEAWAY

Chillies (Chinese and Indian)
39 Park Street
(0117) 927 9484
Chinese and Indian together? Utter genius.

Simply Thai
67 Gloucester Road, Bishopston
(0117) 924 4117
Freshly cooked for you while you wait.

TAKEAWAY PIZZA

Ask Pizza and Pasta
51 Park Street
(0117) 934 9922
Take them away and eat in your own time.

Support

Illustration by Joly Braime

Bristol Royal Infirmary
Marlborough Street
(0117) 923 0000

Bristol University Student Health Service
Hampton House Health Centre
St Michael's Hill
(0117) 330 2720

Bristol University Student Welfare
4th Floor, Students' Union
(0117) 954 5889

Bristol University Nightline
(0117) 926 6266
nightline@bristol.ac.uk

Bristol University Security Services
Royal Fort Lodge
(0117) 928 7848

NHS Direct
(0845) 4647

Redland Police Station
Redland Road
(08454) 567 000

The Samaritans
(08457) 909 090

Southmead Police Station
Southmead Road
(08454) 567 000

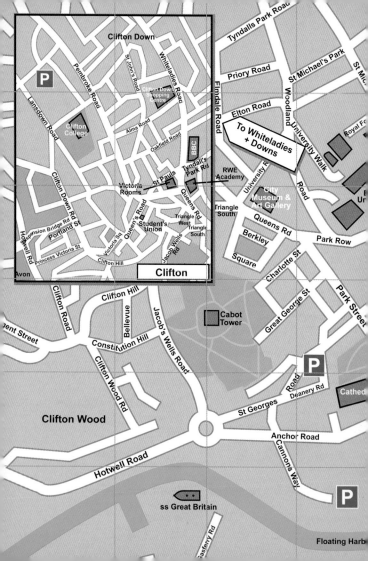

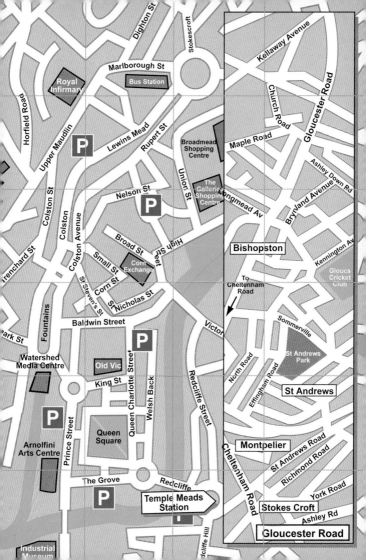

Index

Gazing at the stars

THERE'S NOTHING LIKE A GOOD CELEB SPOT TO MAKE YOUR DAY SEEM MORE EXCITING, SO HERE'S A RUNDOWN OF WHO YOU'RE LIKELY TO SEE IN BRISTOL

Life in the West Country seems to breed humour: **Simon Pegg, Justin Lee Collins, Chris Morris** and **Lee Evans** are just some of the comedians who have lived in Bristol. Little Britain stars **David Walliams and Matt Lucas** met as students at Bristol University, and Matt tested his jokes on the audiences of Jesters Comedy Club before TV glory beckoned. Actor **Jeremy Irons** trained at the Bristol Old Vic Theatre School, supporting himself by busking on the city's streets. Other Old Vic alumni include **Helen Baxendale, Daniel Day-Lewis, Gene Wilder, Patrick Stewart** and Blackadder actor **Tony Robinson**.

The Bristol music scene is represented by **Kosheen, Roni Size, Tricky, Portishead**, and chart topper **James Blunt**, who studied at Bristol University. BBC One's **Casualty** and **Holby City** is also filmed in Bristol, and the stars of the show are rumoured to favour The Coronation Tap for a post-work pint. Among the true Bristolians who started life in the city is actor **Cary Grant** – he was expelled from Fairfield Grammar School in 1918 for investigating the girls' bathroom.